shoots, leaves & eats

First published in Great Britain in 2004 by Cassell Illustrated,
a division of Octopus Publishing Group Limited
2–4 Heron Quays, London E14 4JP

A CIP catalogue record for this book is available from the British Library.

ISBN 1-84403-287-6
EAN 9781844032877

Editor: Joanne Wilson
Design: Design 23
Consultant Editor (Gardening): Andrew Mikolajski
Contributing Editor (Home Economy): Anna Cheifetz,
Cara Frost-Sharratt
Special Photography: Neil Barclay
Index: Indexing Specialists

Printed at Toppan, China

shoots, leaves & eats

CASSELL
ILLUSTRATED

contents

shoots

the freshest veg

salad leaves and spinach

Salad leaves and spinach are fast-maturing crops that can be sown at intervals to produce virtually a continual supply of fresh leaves almost the entire year. To harvest leaves in winter, however, plants need to be grown under cover in cold areas. Growing in containers, such as window boxes and hanging baskets, is recommended, as slug control is much easier. Tie copper bands around the rims of the pots to deter the hungry pests.

Some varieties, such as Lamb's lettuce (corn salad) which is particularly easy to grow, can be grown as a summer or as a winter crop. Keep cutting the leaves to prolong the harvest over several weeks. Rocket has a peppery taste and wild rocket is a delicious variety. Spinach is a rich source of iron, and the young leaves can be eaten raw.

Sow in seed trays with or without modules (compartments) or sow *in situ* – this is best for summer sowings, as transplants tend to wilt in the heat. Thin as recommended for the variety, but don't discard the thinnings as these are great in salads.

Growing from seed: Early spring to autumn.
Soil: Fertile, moisture-retentive soil with good drainage.
Water: Regularly – especially during dry spells.
Conditions: Any sunny, open site sheltered from strong winds. Most lettuces are best sheltered from hot sun in summer. Rocket tolerates shade.
Harvest: Pick leaves in succession, or cut whole plants 5 cm (2 inches) above soil level.
Other: Red lettuces are less attractive to slugs than green varieties.

Grilled Little Gems with Brie and Pine Nuts

Preparation: 10 minutes
Cooking: 8–10 minutes
Serves: 4

handful of pine nuts
2 little gems, cut in half lengthways
2 tablespoons olive oil
4 thick slices farmhouse style bread or ciabatta,
   lightly toasted
1 tablespoon pesto
4 thick slices Brie cheese
4 sun-blush tomatoes

Toast the pine nuts in a frying pan or under the grill, until lightly browned.

Place the little gem halves, cut-side up, in a shallow, heatproof dish and drizzle over the olive oil.

Place under a hot grill for 5–8 minutes. Remove from the heat and arrange each half on a slice of the toasted bread. Spoon over a little pesto, top with the Brie and return to the grill for a couple of minutes, until the cheese begins to melt.

Place a sun-blush tomato on each serving and scatter the pine nuts over. Serve at once.

Spinach and Stilton Bake

Preparation: 15 minutes
Cooking: 1 hour
Serves: 4–6

1.5 kg (3 lb) new potatoes, scrubbed
25 g (1 oz) butter, plus extra for greasing
1.5 kg (3 lb) spinach, washed
2 tablespoons lemon juice
2 tablespoons olive oil
2 onions, peeled and chopped
3 garlic cloves, peeled and crushed
125 g (4 oz) wholewheat flour
2 carrots, scrubbed and grated
1 tablespoon wholegrain mustard
300 ml ($1/2$ pint) milk
300 ml ($1/2$ pint) double cream
250 g (9 oz) Stilton cheese, crumbled
$1/4$ teaspoon grated nutmeg
salt and freshly ground black pepper

Bring a large pan of water to the boil and cook the potatoes until just underdone.
Drain. Leave to cool, then slice. Preheat the oven to 180°C (350°F), Gas Mark 4.

Melt the butter in a large pan and add the spinach leaves, then the lemon juice.
Stir, then cover and cook for 2 minutes until the spinach is wilted. Remove from the heat.

Heat the olive oil in a frying pan and sauté the onions and garlic for 5 minutes.
Stir in the flour and cook for 1 minute. Add the carrots and mustard to the pan, then
add the milk and cream and stir. Continue cooking over a medium heat, stirring until the
sauce has thickened to the consistency of thick cream, then add the Stilton, a bit at a
time. When the cheese has melted, stir in the cooked spinach.

Season the mixture with salt and pepper and turn into a greased ovenproof dish.
Lay the potatoes on top, sprinkle over the nutmeg and cook in the preheated oven for
35 minutes or until the potatoes are browned.

Spinach Gnocchi

Preparation: 15 minutes, plus soaking
Cooking: 10 minutes
Serves: 4

125 g (4 oz) day-old bread, crusts removed
200 ml (7 fl oz) milk
1 1/2 kg (3 lb) baby spinach leaves
1 tablespoon lemon juice
2 eggs, beaten, plus 2 egg yolks
1 1/2 tablespoons single cream
150 g (5 oz) freshly grated Parmesan cheese
4 tablespoons plain flour
100 g (3 1/2 oz) butter

In a shallow dish, cover the bread with the milk, and set aside to soak for 10 minutes.

Place the spinach in a large pan and add the lemon juice. Heat gently and steam the spinach for a few minutes until wilted. Remove and squeeze out all the moisture, then chop the spinach.

In a large bowl, mix the spinach with the beaten eggs and egg yolks, then stir in the cream and half the Parmesan. Squeeze out all the excess moisture from the bread, then add this to the bowl and stir.

Bring a large pan of water to the boil. Form the spinach mixture into small dumplings, sprinkling with a little of the flour, to prevent them sticking.

Carefully drop the dumplings into the pan of boiling water, return to a simmer and cook for 2–3 minutes. When cooked, they should float on the surface and you can remove them with a slotted spoon.

Melt the butter and pour over the dumplings. Sprinkle over the remaining Parmesan and serve.

Four Leaf Salad

Preparation: 10 minutes
Cooking: 4 minutes
Serves: 4

3 eggs
1 iceberg lettuce, leaves roughly torn
2 Lollo Rosso hearts, chopped
200 g (7 oz) Lollo Biondo leaves, roughly torn
200 g (7 oz) Oak leaf lettuce, leaves roughly torn
2 tablespoons chopped parsley
2 tablespoons chopped chives

For the dressing:
$1\frac{1}{2}$ tablespoons mild olive oil
1 tablespoon walnut oil
1 tablespoon lemon juice
$\frac{1}{2}$ tablespoon wholegrain mustard
salt and freshly ground black pepper

Place the eggs in a small pan, cover with cold water and bring to the boil. Cook for about 4 minutes then drain and rinse under cold water to cool, before peeling and cutting into halves.

Place all the dressing ingredients in a screw-top container, seal tightly and shake vigorously to combine.

Arrange the salad leaves in a serving bowl with the eggs, sprinkle over the herbs then drizzle over the dressing. Serve the salad with French bread.

tomatoes

Tomatoes are annual plants that have to be raised from seed every year. You can buy young plants at garden centres for growing on at home, but raising your own plants from seed gives a lot more choice and you can experiment with different varieties. Some are recommended for growing outside while others do better in a greenhouse. It's best to vary your site as tomatoes seem to suck all the goodness out of the soil, so containers or gro-bags are a good idea. Some of the dwarf cherry tomatoes can be grown in hanging baskets or in large wooden planters which look nice up against a wall or on a sunny patio.

Sow seed in warmth in spring. Outdoor varieties can be planted out when all risk of frost has passed. Many varieties need support, so either tie the plants to canes driven into the ground next to the main stem or, in a greenhouse, attach them to strings stretched from the ground to the ceiling. Pinch out the side shoots on tall varieties and, when the plant has reached the top of the cane or string, take out the growing tip. Water tomato plants well and feed with a tomato fertiliser.

Growing from seed: Sow indoors 8–10 weeks before planting out.
Soil: Well-drained, rich in organic matter.
Water: Twice daily, to prevent the soil from drying out (the skins will split if it does).
Conditions: Warm and light, sheltered from strong winds.
Harvest: When ripe.
Other: Pinch out the growing tips of the plant when the first fruits appear.

Gruyère and Chilli Stuffed Tomatoes

Preparation: 25 minutes
Cooking: 40 minutes
Serves: 4

4 large tomatoes
1 slice of bread
3 tablespoons milk
75 g (3 oz) butter
4 shallots, peeled and finely chopped
1 onion, peeled and finely chopped
1 garlic clove, peeled and finely chopped
250 g (9 oz) minced beef
handful of parsley, chopped
220 g (7$1/2$ oz) freshly grated Gruyère cheese
salt and freshly ground black pepper

Preheat the oven to 200°C (400°F), Gas Mark 6. Cut the tops off the tomatoes. Using a teaspoon, scoop out the insides, being careful not to pierce the skins. Reserve the pulp and juice.

Cut the crusts from the bread and soak the bread in the milk. Melt the butter in a pan and fry the shallots, onion and garlic, until softened. Add the mince to the pan and cook for a few minutes. Remove to a bowl and stir through the reserved tomato pulp and juice.

Squeeze the milk from the bread, using your hands. Add the parsley and bread to the mince mixture, season and stir well. Carefully fill the tomatoes with the mixture, adding a little Gruyère to the top of each filled tomato.

Place the tomatoes in an ovenproof dish and transfer to the preheated oven for 30 minutes. Serve immediately with a crisp green salad.

Plum Tomato Tart

Preparation: 25 minutes, plus chilling
Cooking: 1 hour 15 minutes
Serves: 4–6

1.25 kg (2^1/$_2$ lb) vine or plum tomatoes
200 g (7 oz) plain flour, plus extra, for dusting
100 g (3^1/$_2$ oz) butter
100 g (3^1/$_2$ oz) Parmesan cheese, grated
1 egg, beaten
3 tablespoons olive oil
1 red chilli, finely chopped
2 garlic cloves, peeled and crushed
few sprigs thyme
1 tablespoon pesto
salt and freshly ground black pepper

Line a baking tray with baking paper and spread the tomatoes evenly over it. Roast in a preheated oven, 160ºC (325ºF), Gas Mark 3, for 30 minutes.

Meanwhile, in a large bowl, rub the flour and butter together, until you have a mixture that resembles breadcrumbs. Stir in the Parmesan, then add the egg. Mix together well to form a large, round ball, adding a splash of cold water if the mixture is too dry. Tip out onto a floured chopping board and knead gently. Transfer the pastry to a plastic bag and set aside to chill in the fridge for 1 hour.

Remove the pastry and roll it out to fit a 25 cm (10 inch) flan tin with a removeable base. In a large bowl, combine the roasted tomatoes with the olive oil, chilli, garlic and thyme, and season with salt and pepper. Grease the tin and spread the pastry in it.

Using the back of a spoon, spread the pesto thinly over the pastry base. Fill the pastry with the tomato mixture and cook in the preheated oven for 1 hour. If the pastry isn't cooked through, return to the oven for a further 15 minutes. Serve hot or cold, with a green salad.

Cherry Tomato Lasagne

Preparation: 20 minutes
Cooking: 50–60 minutes
Serves: 4–6

2 tablespoons olive oil
2 garlic cloves, peeled and crushed
300 g (10 oz) minced beef or lamb
400 g (13 oz) pasata (sieved tomatoes)
2 teaspoons chopped thyme
100 g (3^1/$_2$ oz) butter, plus extra for greasing
1^1/$_2$ tablespoons flour
450 ml (^{3}/$_4$ pint) milk
250 g (9 oz) mozzarella cheese
6 lasagne sheets
300 g (10 oz) cherry tomatoes, halved
handful of basil leaves, torn
100 g (3^1/$_2$ oz) Parmesan cheese, grated
salt and freshly ground black pepper
1 tablespoon chopped thyme leaves

Heat the olive oil in a large frying pan, add the garlic and cook for 2 minutes. Add the mince and fry for a few minutes, until browned. Add the pasata and thyme to the pan, stir and allow the sauce to begin to simmer. Cook for 5 minutes, then remove from the heat and season with salt and pepper. Preheat the oven to 190°C (375°F), Gas Mark 5.

In a separate pan, melt the butter. Add the flour, stirring vigorously, to make a paste. Continue cooking for 1 minute, then add the milk, a little at a time, stirring to remove any lumps. Reduce the heat to low and add the mozzarella, a little at a time, until the mixture has formed a thick creamy sauce, then remove from the heat.

Grease a 20–25 cm (8–10 inch), deep baking dish. Pour a thin layer of the meat sauce into the dish. Spoon over a layer of the mozzarella sauce, then place a layer of lasagne sheets on top, being careful not to overlap the sheets. Place a layer of cherry tomatoes and basil on top of the pasta, then repeat the layers, in this order, until the ingredients are used up, finishing with a layer of cheese sauce.

Sprinkle over the Parmesan and bake in the oven, for 30–45 minutes, until the sauce is bubbling and the top is browned.

SHOOTS SHOOTS SHOOTS SHOOTS SHOOTS SHOOT

peas and beans

Legumes, or podded vegetables are all are at their best when freshly picked, so home-grown ones are always better than shop-bought ones. Some are good enough to eat raw in salads, and nearly all are easy to grow.

Most peas and beans can be sown *in situ*. In colder areas, you can raise plants under cover for planting out once the worst of the frosts is over. Some beans are climbers that need support – wigwams or lines of canes – but others are dwarf and naturally make neat, compact plants. It's possible to be picking beans from early spring to late autumn by careful choice among the many varieties. Broad beans are the easiest, and some hardy varieties can even be sown in winter. Other beans such as runner beans are fast growing and abundant and will carry on producing almost as long as you keep picking. Sow most varieties 1–3 cm ($1/2$ –1 inches) deep and leave 15 cm (6 inches) between plants (more for climbers).

Growing from seed: Sow broad beans in winter for early crops, peas and other beans from spring to early summer, depending on the variety. They can also be grown in polytunnels for earlier crops.
Soil: Deep dug, moist and fertile soil with good drainage.
Water: Water well in dry spells, as soil should never dry out in growing season.
Conditions: Sunny but sheltered.
Harvest: Mid-summer to early autumn.
Other: Tall climbing beans are susceptible to winds. Do not grow beans on the same site each year.

Braised Peas with Olive Oil

Preparation: 5 minutes, plus soaking
Cooking: 10–25 minutes
Serves: 4 (as a side dish)

400 g (13 oz) freshly shelled peas
75 ml (3 fl oz) olive oil
1 onion, peeled and thinly sliced
1 teaspoon caster sugar
salt and freshly ground black pepper

Soak the peas in cold water for 1 hour. Heat the olive oil in a pan and fry the onion, over a medium heat, until soft and golden.

Drain the peas and add to the pan, along with the sugar. Season with salt and pepper and heat, until the peas are cooked through. (Homegrown peas can take up to 15 minutes, whereas bought varieties tend to be smaller and may only take 5 minutes.) Serve as an accompaniment to roast meat.

Achard de Legumes

Preparation: 20 minutes
Cooking: about 8 minutes
Serves: 4–6

1/4 large white cabbage, shredded
6 carrots, grated
125 g (4 oz) runner beans, thinly sliced
1/4 cauliflower, broken into tiny florets
1 tablespoon olive oil
2 onions, peeled and thinly sliced
handful of peanuts
salt

For the dressing:
2 red chillies, finely chopped
1 1/2 teaspoons mustard seeds, crushed
1 teaspoon curry powder
25 g (1 oz) fresh root ginger, chopped
3 garlic cloves, peeled and crushed
50 ml (2 fl oz) groundnut oil or olive oil
40 ml (1 1/2 fl oz) white wine vinegar
1/2 teaspoon ground turmeric

Bring a large pan of salted water to the boil. Add the cabbage, carrots, beans and cauliflower to the pan and blanch for 2–3 minutes, then drain and place in a serving dish.

In a small bowl, mix together all the dressing ingredients, adding a splash of water, to make a paste.

Heat the olive oil in a large wok or frying pan and fry the onion for 30 seconds. Add the dressing, season with salt and stir-fry for 1 minute. Add the vegetables and peanuts to the wok, mixing well. Stir-fry for 1 minute, then remove from the heat.

Serve with boiled or steamed rice for a main meal, or on its own as a warm salad.

Balti Mixed Vegetables

Preparation: 15 minutes
Cooking: 20–30 minutes
Serves: 4

2–3 tablespoons olive oil
1 small onion, peeled and chopped
1 garlic clove, peeled and crushed
2.5 cm (1 inch) piece of fresh root ginger, grated
1 teaspoon chilli powder
2 teaspoons ground coriander
1/2 teaspoon ground turmeric
500 g (1 lb) diced mixed vegetables such as peas,
    carrots, cauliflower, swede
2–3 tomatoes, skinned and chopped
salt

Heat the oil in a large wok or heavy-based saucepan and gently fry the onion for
5–10 minutes or until lightly browned. Add the garlic, ginger, chilli powder, coriander,
turmeric and a pinch of salt. Fry for 2–3 minutes, add the diced vegetables and stir-fry
for a further 2–3 minutes.

Add the chopped tomatoes. Stir well and add a little water. Cover and cook for
10–12 minutes, or until the vegetables are tender, adding a little more water, if
necessary, to prevent the vegetables sticking to the bottom of the wok.

Serve at once with chapatis or naan bread.

asparagus

Asparagus is a perennial, and to grow it you need to make a dedicated asparagus bed that's a permanent fixture. The succulent spears that thrust through the soil are well worth the small amount of trouble involved.

To ensure crops of uniform quality, it's best to buy plants rather than growing from seed. They are usually sold in early spring, as 'crowns' that are still dormant or just coming into growth, and it's important to plant them as quickly as possible to prevent them from drying out.

Dig trenches 20 cm (8 inches) deep and 30 cm (12 inches) wide. Make a ridge of soil along the middle of each trench 10 cm (4 inches) high. Place the asparagus crowns on top of the ridge with the roots trailing to either side, to aid drainage. Fill the trenches to the level of the crowns. Mound up the soil as the plants grow, so that there is only ever about 10 cm (4 inches) of stem above soil level. The plants take some time to establish, so crop them only lightly the year after planting, cutting the spears up to 5 cm (2 inches) below ground level.

Soil: Moderately fertile. Good drainage is essential.
Water: Water young plants frequently to ensure they establish well.
Conditions: Sunny and open site, but not exposed.
Harvest: Late spring to early summer.
Other: Cut back the yellowing foliage in autumn.

Little Asparagus Tartlets

Preparation: 25 minutes, plus chilling
Cooking: about 35 minutes
Serves: 5

For the pastry:
50 g (2 oz) soft butter, at room temperature
100 g (3^1/2 oz) plain flour
^{1}/2 teaspoon paprika
1 tablespoon poppy seeds
40 g (1^1/2 oz) Cheddar cheese

^{3}/4 tablespoon olive oil
100 g (3^1/2 oz) asparagus tips, chopped into 2.5 cm (1 inch) pieces
100 g (3^1/2 oz) Gruyère cheese, grated
6 eggs, 1 beaten, the rest left whole
50 g (2 oz) Parmesan cheese, finely grated
salt and freshly ground black pepper

Make the pastry by rubbing the butter into the flour, then adding the paprika, poppy seeds and Cheddar. Add enough cold water to make a dough, (about 2 tablespoons) then transfer the pastry to a plastic bag and set aside in the fridge for 30 minutes, to chill.

You will need five 10 cm (4 inches) pastry or quiche tins. Remove the pastry from the fridge and roll out thinly on a floured surface. Turn the pastry tins upside down and use them to make five rounds in the pastry, leaving 2.5 cm (1 inch) between the rim of the pastry tin and the edge of the circle.

Carefully line the tins with the pastry and bake in the preheated oven, 180°C (350°F), Gas Mark 4, for 15 minutes. Remove from the oven, brush the bases and sides with beaten egg, then return to the oven for a further 5 minutes.

Heat the olive oil in a frying pan and fry the asparagus tips for about 3–5 minutes, until tender, then divide them between the pastry cases. Sprinkle over the Gruyère and break one egg into each pastry case. Sprinkle over the Parmesan and return to the oven for 12–15 minutes. Season and serve immediately with a salad garnish.

Penne with Fava Beans, Asparagus and Mint

Preparation: 10 minutes
Cooking: about 15 minutes
Serves: 4

300 g (10 oz) dried, penne pasta
500 g (1 lb) asparagus, trimmed and cut into 5 cm (2 inch) lengths
2 tablespoons olive oil
250 g (9 oz) fresh fava beans
75 ml (3 fl oz) crème fraîche
125 g (4 oz) grated Parmesan cheese, plus extra to garnish
25 g (1 oz) mint, chopped, plus extra to garnish
salt and freshly ground black pepper

Bring a pan of lightly salted water to the boil, then add the pasta, return to the boil and cook for 10 minutes or according to the packet instructions. In a separate pan, steam the asparagus in a little water for 5 minutes, then remove and drain. Place on a lightly greased baking sheet, brush with olive oil and place under a preheated, moderate grill for 6 minutes. Turn occasionally.

Cook the fava beans in lightly salted, boiling water for 2 minutes, or until tender, then drain. Drain the pasta, pour the crème fraîche into the empty pan and add the beans, asparagus, Parmesan and mint. Heat through, stir into the pasta, season with salt and pepper and serve immediately, garnished with extra Parmesan and mint.

Asparagus Bruschetta

Preparation: 10 minutes
Cooking: 10–15 minutes
Serves: 4

150 g (5 oz) asparagus, woody ends trimmed
3 tablespoons olive oil
8 slices ciabatta bread
3 garlic cloves, peeled and crushed
1 tablespoon balsamic vinegar
25 g (1 oz) Parmesan cheese shavings
sea salt and freshly ground black pepper

Place the asparagus on a griddle pan and brush with 2 tablespoons of the olive oil. Season with sea salt and pepper and cook, over a medium heat, for 6–8 minutes, turning during cooking.

Meanwhile, toast the ciabatta bread on both sides under a hot grill. Remove, rub with the garlic and drizzle over the remaining olive oil.

Place the cooked asparagus on the toasted ciabatta, sprinkle with balsamic vinegar and Parmesan shavings, and serve immediately.

Soy and Wasabi Asparagus

Preparation: 15 minutes
Cooking: 10 minutes
Serves: 4–6 (as a side dish)

500 g (1 lb) asparagus, woody ends trimmed
1 bunch of spring onions
1–2 tablespoons sesame seeds, toasted
sea salt and freshly ground black pepper

For the dressing:
5 cm (2 inch) piece of fresh root ginger, peeled and grated
5 tablespoons soy sauce
juice of 1 lemon
1–2 teaspoons wasabi, (according to taste)
75 ml (3 fl oz) olive oil

Scrape or peel the bottom of the asparagus spears. Cut each spear into 3 equal lengths, keeping the tips to one side.

Bring a little water to the boil in a large pan and steam the stem pieces of the asparagus for 3–5 minutes, until tender. Remove and dry on kitchen paper. Add the tips to the steamer and cook for 2 minutes, then remove and dry.

In a large bowl, mix together the ginger, soy sauce, lemon juice and 1 teaspoon of wasabi. Whisk in the olive oil, a little at a time, then add more wasabi, according to taste. Add the asparagus and spring onions to the bowl and coat thoroughly with half the dressing.

Transfer the asparagus to a serving dish and drizzle over the remaining dressing. Sprinkle over the sesame seeds and serve, with finger bowls and with the sea salt and pepper in separate bowls.

courgettes, cucumber and squash

These plants are members of the cucurbit family, producing fleshy fruits that can be eaten raw – as in the case of cucumbers – or cooked in a variety of ways. Courgette flowers can also be eaten, but don't cut them all or there will be no fruits to follow. Some pumpkins and squashes have a long shelf-life, so you can keep them for several weeks after picking. All can be grown outdoors, but some cucumber varieties are best kept under cover in frost-prone areas.

Sow the seed in spring, in twos or threes in small pots or modules. After germination, remove the weaker seedlings. Grow them on for planting out once the danger of night frosts has passed – when you can also sow *in situ*. Pick courgettes while they are small or they will turn into marrows. All these plants need regular watering if the crops are to develop evenly.

Growing from seed: Sow from spring to early summer, or earlier if under cover, and transplant once all danger of frost has passed.
Soil: Fertile, well-drained soil.
Water: Regularly and frequently.
Conditions: Sun, with shelter from strong winds.
Harvest: Pick courgettes when they are approximately 10 cm (4 inches) long, while pumpkins and cucumbers should be left on the plant until they are ripe.
Other: Protect young plants from slugs and snails.

Thai Butternut Squash Soup

Preparation: 10 minutes
Cooking: about 40 minutes
Serves: 4

3 tablespoons olive oil
$1/2$ large butternut squash, peeled and cut into 5 cm (2 inch) chunks
1 onion, peeled and chopped
1–2 green chillies (according to taste), deseeded and chopped
600 ml (1 pint) vegetable stock
1 x 400 ml (14 fl oz) can coconut milk
handful of fresh coriander, chopped

Heat the oil in a large pan and fry the butternut, onion and chillies for 4 minutes, until the onion is softened.

Add the stock to the pan, stir and simmer, covered, for 30 minutes, or until the pieces of butternut are soft and some of the stock has evaporated (you don't want to discard any liquid at the end).

Add the coconut milk and simmer for 5 more minutes. Serve garnished with the chopped coriander.

Pumpkin Chilli

Preparation: 15 minutes
Cooking: about 50 minutes
Serves: 4–6

$1/2$ medium pumpkin, about 1 kg (2 lb), peeled and diced
$1 1/2$ tablespoons olive oil
1 onion, peeled and chopped
1 garlic clove, peeled and crushed
1 red pepper, cored, deseeded and diced
500 g (1 lb) minced beef
500 g (1 lb) chopped fresh tomatoes
250 ml (9 fl oz) pasata (sieved tomatoes)
425 g (14 oz) can kidney beans, drained and rinsed
1 x 250 g (9 oz) can sweetcorn, drained
3–4 green chillies, deseeded and chopped (according to taste)
$1/2$ tablespoon chilli powder
1 teaspoon ground cumin
handful of parsley, chopped
salt and freshly ground black pepper

Place the pumpkin in a large ovenproof dish and bake in a preheated oven, 160°C (325°F), Gas Mark 3, for 30 minutes.

Heat the olive oil in a large pan and sauté the onion, garlic and pepper for 5 minutes, or until tender. Add the mince to the pan and cook, stirring, until browned. Add the pumpkin and the remaining ingredients, except the parsley, and bring to the boil. Reduce the heat, cover, and simmer for 30 minutes, stirring frequently.

Season with salt and pepper, to taste, and sprinkle over the chopped parsley. Serve with boiled or steamed rice.

Thai Fish Cakes with Cucumber Relish

Preparation: 20 minutes
Cooking: 5 minutes
Serves: 4–6

1 kg (2 lb) white fish fillets such as cod or haddock
1 egg, beaten
2 tablespoons chopped fresh coriander
4 tablespoons red curry paste
1 bunch spring onions, finely chopped
plenty of vegetable oil for deep-frying
2 red chillies, deseeded and chopped into ribbons

For the cucumber relish:
4 tablespoons rice vinegar
4 tablespoons water
50 g (2 oz) sugar
1 pickled garlic clove
1 cucumber, quartered and sliced
4 shallots, finely chopped
1 tablespoon finely chopped ginger

Place the fish, egg, coriander and curry paste in a food processor, or blend using a hand-held blender until well-combined. Add the spring onions to the mixture, stirring well.

Shape the mixture into approximately 20 small balls and flatten to make fishcakes.

Add enough vegetable oil to the wok so that it is deep enough to fry the cakes, two or three at a time. Heat the oil. When hot, add the cakes and cook for a few minutes, until brown. Remove to paper towels to absorb any excess oil.

Make the relish by bringing the vinegar, water and sugar to the boil, stirring as the sugar dissolves. Remove and allow to cool. Combine the remaining ingredients in a bowl and pour the vinegar mixture on top. Serve with the fish cakes at once.

Griddled Courgette Salad

Preparation: 10 minutes, plus cooling
Cooking: about 10 minutes
Serves: 4

6 tablespoons olive oil
6 courgettes, sliced lengthways
2 tablespoons lemon juice
$1/2$ tablespoon sugar
3 tablespoons chopped marjoram
salt and freshly ground black pepper

Heat 2 tablespoons of the olive oil, in a heavy-based griddle pan. When hot, add the
courgette slices to the pan in batches, pressing them down with a spatula to create
griddle marks. When browned, turn the slices over and cook the other side in the same
way. Remove from the heat and set aside.

In a small bowl, mix together the lemon juice with the remaining olive oil, the sugar,
marjoram and season with salt and pepper.

Place the courgettes on a serving dish and drizzle over the dressing. Allow to cool or
serve hot with couscous or steamed rice.

onions and garlic

Both onions and shallots are essential to the cook. Shallots are smaller and sweeter in flavour than onions and make a useful alternative. You can grow both from seed, but it's easier to buy sets – small bulbs that have been heat-treated to ward off disease. For cropping in autumn, plant in spring, about 15 cm (6 inches) apart. For a spring crop, plant Japanese onions, which are hardier, in late summer. If you want to store onions, dry them off first, either in the sun or hung up in a dry shed.

Garlic needs a long growing season, and a period of cold, so ideally plant bulbs in late autumn – though you may get away with a spring planting. Split a mature garlic head into individual cloves and plant them about 15 cm (6 inches) apart. You can use garlic bought from a supermarket or grocer, but for the best results buy from a proper nursery. Dig up the bulbs the following summer, then dry them off for storage.

Plant: Onions: late summer/early autumn for early crops; early to mid-spring for maincrop. Garlic: autumn through to early spring.
Soil: Light, but firm, fertile and well-drained.
Water: Water during dry spells.
Conditions: Full sun but with some shelter from strong winds.
Harvest: See above. To store, lift the bulbs only when the leaves have died down.
Other: Do not grow onions in the same soil each year.

Red Onion Ciabatta Burgers

Preparation: 20 minutes, plus chilling
Cooking: 16–20 minutes
Makes: 6

For the burgers:
500 g (1 lb) minced beef
2 tablespoons peeled and finely chopped red onion
50 g (2 oz) breadcrumbs
1 egg, lightly beaten
1 tablespoon soy sauce or Worcestershire sauce
salt and freshly ground black pepper

flour, for dusting
2 tablespoons oil for frying
12 strips Pancetta
6 ciabatta rolls
1 avocado, peeled and sliced
handful of rocket leaves

In a large bowl, mix together all the ingredients for the burgers. Flour your hands and form the mixture into 8 burger shapes. Set aside in the fridge for 1 hour, to chill.

When ready to cook, sprinkle the burgers with flour, heat the oil in a large frying pan and fry the burgers, over a medium heat, for 8–10 minutes on each side. After turning, place the Pancetta strips next to the burgers in the pan.

Split the rolls and layer the avocado and rocket on the bottom. Fill each roll with a burger and a strip of Pancetta and serve.

Roast Onion, Gorgonzola and Walnut Pizza

Preparation: 20 minutes, plus rising
Cooking: 45 minutes
Serves: 4

For the dough:
1 teaspoon dry active yeast
150 ml (5 fl oz) warm water
pinch of caster sugar
250 g (9 oz) strong white flour, plus extra for dusting
1 teaspoon salt
1 tablespoon extra virgin olive oil

For the topping:
3 onions, peeled and cut into 8 wedges
3 tablespoons extra virgin olive oil, plus extra to drizzle
2 tablespoons chopped sage
1 tablespoon balsamic vinegar
175 g (6 oz) Gorgonzola cheese, crumbled
4 tablespoons crème fraîche
40 g (1 1/2 oz) shelled walnuts, roughly chopped
salt and freshly ground pepper

Stir the yeast into the water until dissolved. Stir in the sugar, 4 tablespoons of the flour and leave in a warm place for 10 minutes. When ready, sift the remaining flour into a bowl, add the salt, stir and make a well in the centre. Pour in the frothy yeast mixture and the oil and combine to form a soft dough. Knead for 8–10 minutes on a lightly floured surface. Shape the dough into a ball and place in an oiled bowl. Cover with oiled clingfilm and leave to rise in a warm place for 1 hour or until doubled in size.

Meanwhile place the onion in a shallow roasting dish, top with the sage and season well with salt and pepper. Drizzle over the olive oil and roast for 20–30 minutes. Add the vinegar and continue to cook for 5 minutes. Leave to cool.

In a large bowl mix together the Gorgonzola and crème fraiche.

Divide the dough into four and roll out each ball to make a 23 cm (9 inch) round. Transfer the bases to baking sheets and top each with a quarter of the onions, cheese, the remaining sage and walnuts. Season with pepper and drizzle with a little oil. Bake for 10–12 minutes until the bases are crisp.

Lamb with Garlic and Red Wine

Preparation: 15 minutes, plus marinating
Cooking: 8–12 minutes (12–16 minutes for chops)
Serves: 4

For the marinade:
200 ml (7 fl oz) red wine
3 garlic cloves, peeled and crushed
few rosemary, marjoram and mint sprigs
1 tablespoon olive oil

For the garlic mayonnaise:
4 tablespoons mayonnaise
1 garlic clove, peeled and crushed
$1/2$ tablespoon mint, chopped

8 lamb cutlets or chops
2 tablespoons clear honey

In a small bowl, mix together the ingredients for the marinade. Place the lamb in a
large dish and pour over the marinade. Cover and set aside in the fridge for 1–2 hours.
  In a small bowl, mix together the ingredients for the garlic mayonnaise.
  Remove the lamb from the fridge and place in a heatproof dish. Drizzle over
the honey, place under a hot grill and cook for 8–12 minutes, if using cutlets, or
2–16 minutes, if using chops. Turn the lamb over halfway during cooking.
  Serve each cutlet with a spoonful of garlic mayonnaise, boiled new potatoes and
steamed green vegetables.

beetroot, carrots and turnips

These root crops are annuals that are simple to grow and vastly superior in taste to those you find in the supermarket. Some varieties produce crops in a matter of weeks. Carrots do best sown *in situ*, as they do not transplant well, though you could try starting off early varieties in modules. Thin the seedlings to 7 cm (3 inches) apart. Growing carrots among onions or leeks is said to deter carrot root fly – the only serious pest.

Growing from seed: Early spring–mid-summer, depending on variety.
Sow on an overcast day to reduce the risk of carrot-fly.
Soil: Light and fertile with good drainage; sandy soils are good.
Water: Do not overwater.
Conditions: Open site but sheltered from the worst of the weather.
Harvest: Late spring onwards.
Other: Maincrop varieties can be left in the ground and lifted as required until frost threatens.

Turnips are fast growing, and can be harvested as early soon as sixty days after sowing. The leaves (sometimes called turnip tops) are also edible. You can sow *in situ*, thinning to up to 15 cm (6 inches). Turnips are best when small and young. Don't leave them in the soil too long or the roots will turn woody.

Growing from seed: Early spring to late summer.
Soil: Light to medium, reliably moist.
Water: Do not let the soil dry out, but too much watering reduces flavour.
Conditions: Open but with protection; they will take some shade.
Harvest: 6–10 weeks from sowing.
Other: gently pull them from the soil by their leaves.

Beetroot can also be sown *in situ* in spring. Thin the seedlings to up to 10 cm (4 inches) apart. The young leaves can be eaten raw in salads or lightly cooked, and you can harvest the roots from 7 weeks after sowing onwards, depending on the size you want. They can be boiled, baked or pickled.

Growing from seed: Spring.
Soil: Light, fertile soil with good drainage.
Water: Only in hot, dry periods with little rain.
Conditions: Sunny, open site. They grow best in cool conditions.
Harvest: 12–14 weeks from planting. Early summer through to late autumn.
Other: Baby beets are simply beetroot harvested while the roots are still small.

Vegetable Terrine

Preparation: 25 minutes, plus chilling
Cooking: 15 minutes
Serves: 4–6

2 tablespoons olive oil
100 g (3^1/$_2$ oz) baby corn
125 g (4 oz) spinach leaves, thick stalks removed
1 medium carrot, peeled and finely chopped
2 small courgettes, cut into thin rounds
100 g (3^1/$_2$ oz) trimmed French beans
400 ml (14 fl oz) pasata (sieved tomatoes)
1–2 teaspoons Worcestershire sauce
1 packet unflavoured gelatine
50 g (2 oz) Parmesan cheese, grated
1 small bunch basil
2 tablespoons pesto
salt and freshly ground black pepper

Brush a 23 x 12 cm (9 x 5 inch) loaf tin with olive oil, then line with clingfilm, allowing some to overhang the sides. Brush the insides with oil.

Bring a little water to the boil in a pan and steam the corn for 6 minutes. Remove the corn, then steam the spinach, until wilted. In a separate pan, steam the carrot, courgette and beans for about 3 minutes, until just tender. When all the vegetables are cooked, rinse under cold running water, then spread out to dry on paper towels. Cut the corn in half lengthways.

In a small pan, heat the pasata, then add the Worcestershire sauce and gelatine, stirring, so it dissolves. Add the Parmesan, season with salt and pepper, then let the mixture cool to room temperature.

Line the loaf tin with three-quarters of the spinach. Tear the basil and scatter half over the spinach. Layer the vegetables alternately, spooning a little tomato sauce, pesto and more basil over each layer. Finish with tomato, pesto and lastly the remaining spinach and cover with the overhanging clingfilm. Place in the fridge for 4–5 hours, to chill. When ready to serve, unfold the clingfilm from the top and invert the terrine onto a plate, carefully removing the clingfilm from around the sides.

Honeyed Carrots

Preparation: 10 minutes
Cooking: 15 minutes
Serves: 4

200 g (7 oz) carrots, peeled and cut into julienne strips
4 tablespoons olive oil
1 1/2 tablespoons clear honey
2 tablespoons wholegrain mustard

Preheat the oven to 180°C (350°F), Gas Mark 4. Bring a large pan of salted water to the boil, add the carrots and simmer gently, uncovered, for 3 minutes. Drain and remove. In a small bowl, mix together the remaining ingredients.

Place the carrots in a large bowl and drizzle over half the dressing, mixing gently to coat all over. Using a slotted spoon, transfer the carrots to a roasting tin. Cook in the preheated oven, 180°C (350°F), Gas Mark 4, for about 15 minutes.

In a small pan, gently heat the remaining dressing. When the carrots are cooked, remove from the oven, transfer to a serving dish and drizzle over the warm dressing. Serve with roast meat or mashed potatoes.

Baby Turnip and Beetroot Risotto

Preparation: 10 minutes
Cooking: 30 minutes
Serves: 4

50 g (2 oz) unsalted butter
1 onion, peeled and finely chopped
5 baby turnips, roughly chopped
5 green turnip tops, washed and shredded (optional)
350 g (12^1/$_2$ oz) Arborio rice
1 small beetroot
green tops from beetroot, washed and shredded (optional)
up to 2 litres (3^1/$_2$ pints) chicken or vegetable stock, kept simmering
50 g (2 oz) freshly grated Parmigiano Reggiano cheese
salt and freshly ground black pepper

Bake the beetroot in its skin, for 1^1/$_2$–2 hours at 150°C (300°F), Gas Mark 2.

Melt half the butter in a large pan and fry the onion and the turnip until soft. Add the rice and stir, cooking gently for about 4 minutes, until the rice grains are heated through. Scrape out all the flesh from the baked beetroot and add to the pan, stirring.

Stir in 3 ladlefuls of stock, cooking, until the rice has absorbed most of the liquid. Continue to add the stock, 1 ladleful at a time, stirring to allow the rice to absorb the liquid before adding more. When all but a ladleful of stock is left, add the shredded turnip tops, and continue to cook the risotto.

When tender but firm to the bite, remove the pan of rice from the heat and stir in the remaining butter. Season with plenty of salt and pepper and add half the grated Parmigiano Reggiano; then cover and leave to rest for 4 minutes. Stir in another half-ladleful of stock and transfer to warmed serving dishes.

Serve at once, with the remaining cheese sprinkled on top.

Chilli Ginger Carrots and Cauliflower

Preparation: 10 minutes
Cooking: about 12 minutes
Serves: 4–6

6 medium carrots, peeled and sliced into rounds
200 g (7 oz) cauliflower florets
mild olive oil, for frying
2 garlic cloves, peeled and finely sliced
2 small onions, peeled and finely sliced
4 spring onions, sliced into 2.5 cm (1 inch) lengths
1 tablespoon soy sauce
dash of fish sauce
1 red chilli, deseeded and finely chopped
1 teaspoon ground fresh ginger

Bring a pan of water to the boil and cook the carrots and cauliflower for about
3 minutes, then drain and set aside.

Heat the olive oil in a large wok or frying pan and cook the garlic for 1 minute, then
add the onions and cook for 2 minutes, until soft. Add the spring onions, soy and fish
sauces, carrots, and cauliflower to the wok, and stir-fry for 2–3 minutes.

Finally, add the chilli and ginger to the wok and stir-fry for a further 2 minutes.
Serve immediately, with rice or noodles.

Vegetable Crisps

Preparation: 10 minutes
Cooking: 10 minutes
Serves: 4–6 (as a snack)

groundnut oil, for deep-frying
1 carrot, peeled and thinly sliced
2 parsnips, peeled and thinly sliced
2 beetroot, skins removed and cut into thin rounds
1 sweet potato, peeled and thinly sliced
sea salt, for sprinkling

Half fill a wok or large frying pan with groundnut oil and heat for a few minutes, until the oil is hot.

Carefully place the sliced vegetables in the wok and deep-fry in batches for about 3 minutes, until golden and crisp. Cook the parsnips first, then the carrots, sweet potato and finally the beetroot. This will stop the beetroot colour seeping into the others.

Remove with a slotted spoon and place on kitchen paper to absorb the excess oil. Lightly sprinkle over sea salt. Serve as an accompaniment to drinks, or as a snack.

Baby Beetroot, Walnut and Feta Salad

Preparation: 25 minutes
Cooking: 20 minutes
Serves: 4

250 g (9 oz) baby beetroot
2 cos lettuces
handful of chives, snipped
handful of mint leaves, torn
handful of tarragon leaves, chopped
50 g (2 oz) walnut halves, roughly chopped
200 g (7 oz) feta cheese
2 teaspoons clear honey
2 tablespoons lemon juice
6 tablespoons walnut oil
1 tablespoon roughly chopped dill
salt and freshly ground black pepper

Wash the beetroot under cold water and twist off the leaves. Put the beetroot in a pan and cover with water. Bring to the boil and simmer for 20 minutes or until tender, then drain and remove the skin. Chop the beetroot roughly and place in a bowl with the lettuce leaves, chives, mint, tarragon, walnut and feta. Mix together.

Mix the honey, lemon juice, dill and walnut oil in a bowl and season, before drizzling over the salad. Divide and serve.

Beetroot Soup

Preparation: 15 minutes
Cooking: 30–35 minutes
Serves: 4–6

1 tablespoon olive oil
1 onion, peeled and chopped
1 large potato, peeled and diced
500 g (1 lb) beetroot, cooked, skinned and diced
900 ml (1 $\frac{1}{2}$ pints) water
1 tablespoon wholegrain mustard
juice of $\frac{1}{2}$ lemon
salt and freshly ground black pepper

Heat the oil in a large saucepan, add the onion and sauté over a medium heat for 5 minutes, until soft. Add the potato to the pan and cook, covered, for 10 minutes, stirring frequently.

Add the beetroot, water and mustard to the pan, bring to the boil and simmer for 15–20 minutes, or until the potato is soft. Transfer the mixture to a blender or food processor and blend until smooth.

Add lemon juice to taste and season with salt and pepper. Reheat the soup and serve garnished with a little soured cream and some chopped chives.

This soup is equally delicious served chilled.

cabbage, cauliflower and broccoli

Cabbages, a rich source of iron, can be grown year-round, and some of the purple-leaved forms are often grown as ornamentals. If you are growing to eat, however, white cabbages can be eaten raw as the basis of coleslaw. Spring cabbages need only the minimum cooking, while winter cabbages are superb braised slowly in the oven, studded with cloves or spices to enhance their flavour. Cabbages love rich soil, so prepare the site well by digging in plenty of compost or manure before planting. Plant seedlings out about 5 weeks after sowing, when they are large enough to handle. The planting distance varies according to the variety, but is usually 25 cm (10 inches) or more. Protect the young plants from slugs and snails.

Growing from seed: Spring to summer, depending on variety, in trays.
Soil: Fertile, humus-rich soil, but do not plant in ground that has only recently been manured.
Water: Keep moist during dry spells.
Conditions: Full sun, open conditions.
Harvest: Dependent on variety (see above).
Other: Do not grow cabbages in the same part of the garden every year.

Cauliflowers are annuals. The familiar ones have creamy heads (or curds), but there are also tasty dwarf varieties with domed, greenish heads, which are quicker to mature. They tend not to do well during hot, dry summers. Early sowings are best made under cover and transplanted later, when you can also be sowing a second crop *in situ*. Planting distance depends on the variety, later-maturing types typically needing more space. If you've sown for a winter crop, you may need to protect the creamy heads (or curds) from frost by wrapping the leaves around them and tieing them with soft string. Take care not to damage the curds when cutting them from the plant. They can be frozen, but are best eaten as soon as possible.

Growing from seed: Through spring, depending on variety.
Soil: Fertile, moisture-retentive.
Water: Water regularly throughout the growing season.
Conditions: Sheltered from strong winds and frosts.
Harvest: 8–9 months after planting. Cut through the stem of the plant carefully.
Other: Do not grow cauliflowers in the same ground every year.

Broccoli, or calabrese, is one of the best annual green vegetables, and is celebrated for its health-giving properties. Keep picking the young florets – actually the stalks of unopened flowers – and the plants will carry on producing for several weeks. Varieties are classified as early, mid-season and late. Sow the seed either *in situ* or, for early sowings, in modules indoors. Plant these out about 5–6 weeks later. Keep the growing plants well watered and you will be able to start harvesting the florets within about 12–14 weeks.

Growing from seed: Sow in succession from spring to early summer.
Soil: Fertile and moisture-retentive.
Water: Make sure the soil does not dry out during the growing season.
Conditions: Sunny but not too hot.
Harvest: Cut the central, large floret first, before the flowers open. This encourages side-shoots to develop. Cutting these later can result in further flower production.
Other: Do not grow broccoli in the same soil each year.

Braised Red Cabbage

Preparation: 10 minutes
Cooking: 1 hour 10 minutes
Serves: 6 (as a side dish)

1 small red cabbage, approximately 875 g (1³/₄ lb)
2 tablespoons butter
1 medium onion, peeled and chopped
1 cooking apple, peeled, cored and chopped
3 tablespoons red wine
1 tablespoon brown sugar
1/4 teaspoon nutmeg
1 teaspoon salt
3 cloves
handful of raisins
100 ml (3¹/₂ fl oz) water

Preheat the oven to 150°C (300°F), Gas Mark 2. Remove and discard the tough outer leaves of the cabbage then quarter it, remove the stalk and finely chop.

Heat the butter in a frying pan, over a medium heat, until hot. Gently fry the onion and apple for 3 minutes. Add the cabbage to the pan and fry for 2 minutes, then add the remaining ingredients, mixing well to combine.

Pour the contents of the pan into a casserole dish, cover, and cook in the preheated oven for 1 hour. Halfway through cooking, check there is sufficient liquid in the dish and that the cabbage has not stuck to the bottom. If you find the liquid has evaporated, add a little more water.

The cabbage is cooked when it is tender and a dark colour. Braised cabbage is traditionally served with gammon, but is also delicious with beef or roast chicken.

Cabbage Noodle Salad

Preparation: 15 minutes, plus marinating
Serves: 4

1 head white cabbage, thinly sliced
2 packets dried egg noodles, crumbled
6 large spring onions, sliced
1 tablespoon sesame seeds
125 g (4 oz) sliced almonds

For the dressing:
125 ml (4 fl oz) olive oil
2 tablespoons lemon juice
2 tablespoons caster sugar
1 $1/2$ tablespoons soy sauce
2 tablespoons mixed Thai spice
$1/2$ teaspoon salt (optional)

In a large bowl, mix all the salad ingredients together. In a separate bowl, mix the dressing ingredients together and pour about two-thirds of the dressing over the salad. Set aside in the fridge to marinate for 5–6 hours, or overnight.

When ready to serve, remove from the fridge and sprinkle on the remaining dressing. Serve with chicken dishes or as part of a vegetarian meal. The salad is also delicious served with barbecued meat or fish.

Spicy Cauliflower Risotto

Preparation: 10 minutes
Cooking: about 25–30 minutes
Serves: 4

3 tablespoons extra virgin olive oil
$1/2$ small red onion, peeled and finely chopped
3 large garlic cloves, peeled and chopped
2 salted anchovies, finely chopped
$1/4$ teaspoon chilli powder
$1/2$ mild red chilli, deseeded and chopped
1 large sardine, boned and chopped
$1/2$ small cauliflower head, broken into small florets
300 g (10 oz) Arborio rice
dash of white wine vinegar
1.5 litres ($2^1/2$ pints) vegetable stock
1 tablespoon raisins
$1/2$ tablespoon capers
2 sachets of saffron
salt and freshly ground black pepper

Heat the olive oil in a large pan and fry the onion, garlic, anchovies, chilli powder, chopped chilli and sardine for 3–4 minutes. Add the cauliflower and 2 tablespoons of water and cook for 5–10 minutes, before adding the rice, stirring well to coat all the grains. Add the white wine vinegar and stir, then add 2 ladlefuls of stock, the raisins and capers. Cook, stirring, until the liquid has been absorbed.

Continue to add the stock, a ladleful at a time, and cook, stirring, until it has all been absorbed and the rice becomes coated in creamy sauce. This will take about 15–20 minutes. Season well, mix in the saffron, then cover and set aside for 5 minutes, before serving.

Broccoli and Red Leicester Tart

Preparation: 30 minutes, plus chilling
Cooking: 1 hour 15 minutes
Serves: 4–6

For the pastry:
425 g (14 oz) wholewheat flour
$1/2$ teaspoon salt
275 g (10 oz) frozen vegetable margarine, chopped into slithers
2 tablespoons lemon juice

250 g (9 oz) broccoli
2 tablespoons olive oil
1 onion, peeled and finely chopped
2 tablespoons chopped dill
50 g (2 oz) butter, plus extra for greasing
50 g (2 oz) wholewheat flour
300 ml ($1/2$ pint) milk
250 g (9 oz) Red Leicester cheese
3 tablespoons soured cream
pinch of salt
4 eggs, beaten

Preheat the oven to 160ºC (325ºF), Gas Mark 3. Combine the flour and the salt in a bowl and stir in the margarine. Add the lemon juice and enough cold water (125–150 ml / 4–5 fl oz) to make a sticky dough, mixing well. Turn out onto a floured surface, and knead gently. Set aside in a bag in the fridge for 1 hour. Remove and knead for a further 5 minutes to make a smooth dough.

Steam the broccoli in a pan for 3–4 minutes, then drain and rinse. Heat the olive oil in a pan, add the onion and cook until soft. Transfer to a bowl and stir in the dill.

Melt the butter in a pan, add the flour and heat for 2 minutes, stirring constantly. Add a little milk, mixing quickly to break up any lumps. Heat for 2 minutes and add the rest of the milk, stirring often. When smooth, add the soured cream, cheese, salt and eggs.

Grease a quiche dish and roll out the pastry to fill the base and overlap the sides. Trim the excess from the edges. Lay the pastry in the dish and place the broccoli, cooked onions and dill on top of the pastry and pour over the sauce. Bake in the oven for 1 hour. Serve warm or cold, with a rocket salad.

Blue Stilton Cauliflower Cheese

Preparation: 5 minutes
Cooking: 25 minutes
Serves: 4

1 large head of cauliflower, chopped into small florets
2 tablespoons butter
2 tablespoons flour
300 ml (^{1}/$_2$ pint) milk
1 tablespoon Dijon mustard
350 g (12^1/$_2$ oz) blue Stilton cheese

Bring a large pan of water to the boil, add the cauliflower and cook for 5 minutes. Drain, then place the cauliflower in a heatproof dish.

Melt the butter in a pan, over a medium heat. Add the flour and stir to make a paste. Continue stirring for 2 minutes, then gradually add the milk, a little at a time, stirring vigorously. Add the mustard and bring to the boil. Once boiling and starting to thicken, remove from the heat and crumble in most of the Stilton, stirring, to make a thick sauce.

Pour the sauce over the cauliflower, sprinkle over the rest of the Stilton and place under a hot grill for about 10 minutes, until the cheese is bubbling and beginning to brown. Serve with thick crusty bread and a green salad.

peppers and chillies

Sweet peppers (*Capsicum*) and chilli peppers are plants of the tropics and subtropics. To fruit successfully, they need as much sun and warmth as possible, so they are ideal grown in pots or growing bags in a greenhouse or polytunnel. Smaller varieties will flourish on a window-sill.

Sow the seed in warmth from late winter to mid-spring. Prick out the seedlings into small pots, then pot them on into pots of increasing size as they grow. They should make decent-sized plants within 12 weeks, when they can be moved into their final positions. Give them plenty of water and feed with a tomato fertiliser. Taller varieties will need staking, as for tomatoes.

Growing from seed: Late winter to mid-spring in trays of compost.
Soil: Use good-quality potting compost or growing bags.
Water: Water once or twice daily in summer both to wet the compost and to create humidity around the plants.
Conditions: Warmth and light for best fruiting.
Harvest: Mid-summer to early autumn.
Other: Stake taller plants. Watch out for red spider mite and other greenhouse pests if growing under cover.

Hot and Sour Soup

Preparation: 20 minutes
Cooking: about 30 minutes
Serves: 4

1.2 litres (2 pints) chicken stock
2 green chillies, deseeded and chopped
1 teaspoon salt
rind of 1 lime, juice of 3 limes
4 Kaffir lime leaves
3 lemongrass stalks, cut into 2.5 cm (1 inch) pieces
250 g (9 oz) tiger prawns, peeled and shells reserved
250 g (9 oz) scallops, corals removed
2 tablespoons fish sauce
3–4 tablespoons chopped fresh coriander
1 red Serrano chilli, deseeded and finely chopped
6 Shiitake mushrooms, sliced
2 spring onions, sliced

Put the chicken stock in a large, heavy-based pan. Add the green chillies, salt, lime rind, Kaffir lime leaves and lemongrass stalks, and bring to the boil. Reduce the heat, cover and simmer for 20 minutes.

Strain the liquid through a sieve, then return the stock to the pan, discarding what remains. Bring to the boil, then add the prawns and scallops, and cook for 1 minute. Stir in the fish sauce and lime juice, then add the coriander, red chilli, mushrooms and spring onions. Transfer to bowls and serve immediately.

SHOOTS SHOOTS SHOOTS SHOOTS SHOOTS SHOOT

Ginger Chicken and Peppers

Preparation: 20 minutes, plus 15 minutes marinating
Cooking 4–5 minutes
Serves: 4

340 g (^{3}/4 lb) skinless, boneless chicken breasts
1 tablespoon dry sherry
4 spring onions, sliced
2 large carrots, scrubbed and thinly sliced
2 cm (1 inch) piece of root ginger, peeled and finely chopped
1 tablespoon oil
1–2 garlic cloves, peeled and thinly sliced
2 celery stalks, diagonally sliced
1 small green pepper, cored, deseeded and sliced
1 small yellow pepper, cored, deseeded and sliced
2 tablespoons light soy sauce
2 tablespoons lemon juice
grated zest 2 lemons
^{1}/2 teaspoon chilli powder
snipped chives to garnish

Cut the chicken into 8 cm (3 inch) strips. Combine the sherry, spring onions, carrots and ginger, add the chicken strips and toss to coat. Set aside to marinate for 15 minutes.

Heat the oil in a large non-stick frying pan or wok. Add the garlic, celery and green and yellow peppers, and stir-fry for 1 minute. Add the chicken and marinade and cook for 3 minutes. Stir in the soy sauce, lemon juice and zest and chilli powder and cook for 1 more minute.

Divide and serve immediately garnished with chives.

Cashew Chilli Prawns

Preparation: 20 minutes, plus 1 hour marinating
Cooking: 20 minutes
Serves: 4

500 g (1 lb) tiger prawns, shelled and tails removed
6 large spring onions, chopped
90 g (3^1/$_2$ oz) salted cashew nuts
5 tablespoons soy sauce
5 tablespoons white wine or sherry
2 small chillies, deseeded and chopped
1 dried red chilli, deseeded and chopped
2 garlic cloves, peeled and crushed
2 teaspoons grated fresh root ginger
2 tablespoons water
3 tablespoons mild olive oil

In a large bowl, combine the prawns, spring onions and cashew nuts. Stir in the soy sauce, wine or sherry, fresh and dried chillies, garlic, ginger and water. Stir well to combine, then cover and leave to marinate for 1 hour, stirring occasionally.

Heat the oil in a heavy-based frying pan, or wok, and transfer the prawns and sauce to the pan when hot. Cook over a high heat for 4–5 minutes. Serve the prawns with Thai rice.

leeks

Tough and hardy, leeks are an attractive plant, with their pleated fans of grey-green leaves. They are a marvellous crop for autumn and winter and are tasty baked in the oven with pine nuts and a little wine or delicious in stews and soups with a lighter flavour than onions.

Perfect for small gardens, leeks take up little space. They do, however, need a long growing season. You can either start them off in seed trays with modules or sow *in situ*. Either way, they need transplanting when the seedlings have three leaves. Make holes 15–25 cm (6–10 inches) apart in rows, then drop the seedlings in. Water well, then just allow the surrounding soil to collapse in on the plant. This produces leeks with thick, white stems. Mounding up the soil around the base of the leeks up to the lowest leaves as they grow encourages extra length. Harvest from late summer onwards.

Growing from seed: Sow in modules or *in situ* in spring.
Soil: Fertile, well-manured ground.
Water: Water well after planting until established. Keep well watered during prolonged dry spells.
Climate: Full sun, with some shelter from strong winds.
Harvest: When the stems are about 3 cm (1^1/$_2$ inches) thick.
Other: Do not grow leeks in the same ground each year.

Fontina, Gorgonzola and Leek Risotto

Preparation: 10 minutes
Cooking: 25–30 minutes
Serves: 4

40 g (1 1/2 oz) unsalted butter
2 leeks, trimmed and finely chopped
325 g (11 oz) Arborio rice
2 litres (3 1/2 pints) vegetable stock
100 g (3 1/2 oz) Fontina cheese, cut into cubes
100 g (3 1/2 oz) Gorgonzola cheese
25 g (1 oz) freshly grated Parmesan cheese
salt and freshly ground black pepper

Warm half the butter in a large pan, over a medium heat, and gently fry the leeks until soft. Add the rice and cook for 5 minutes, stirring to make sure the grains are coated all over.

Add 2 ladlefuls of the stock and keep stirring, until all the liquid is absorbed. Add the remaining stock, one ladle at a time, stirring and checking the rice to see if it is tender. This will take about 15–20 minutes.

When it is still firm to the bite, but tender, remove the pan from the heat and stir in the three cheeses. Season with salt and pepper and set aside, covered, for a few minutes, until the cheese has melted. Serve with a green salad.

Bacon Cheesey Leeks

Preparation: 10 minutes
Cooking: 1 hour 10 minutes
Serves: 4

4 leeks, washed, trimmed and split lengthways
8 rashers of bacon, grilled

For the sauce:
25 g (1 oz) butter
30 g (1 oz) plain flour
300 ml (^{1}/2 pint) milk
100 g (3^1/2 oz) Cheddar cheese
1 teaspoon mustard
salt and freshly ground black pepper
1 tablespoon chopped fresh parsley

Preheat the oven to 180°C (350°F), Gas Mark 4. Lay the leeks in an oven proof dish, with the cooked bacon on top.

Melt the butter in a pan over a medium heat. Add the flour and stir to make a paste. Continue stirring for 2 minutes, then gradually add the milk, a little at a time, stirring vigorously. Bring to the boil and continue stirring. Once the mixture thickens, remove from the heat.

Stir in most of the cheese, add the mustard and season with salt and pepper.

Pour the cheese sauce over the leeks, sprinkle the remaining cheese on top and bake in the preheated oven for 1 hour.

Divide and serve on its own or with warmed ciabatta bread and tomato salad.

Balsamic Braised Leeks and Peppers

Preparation: 10 minutes
Cooking: 20 minutes
Serves: 4 (as a side dish)

2 tablespoons olive oil
2 leeks, washed, trimmed and cut into 1 cm ($^1/_2$ inch) slices
1 orange pepper, cored, deseeded and chopped
1 red pepper, cored deseeded and chopped
3 tablespoons balsamic vinegar
handful of parsley, chopped
salt and freshly ground black pepper

Heat the oil in a large pan, add the leeks and peppers and stir well to coat, then cook, covered, over a low heat, for 10 minutes.

Add the balsamic vinegar to the pan and cook for a further 10 minutes, until all the liquid has evaporated. Season with salt and pepper and stir in the parsley. Serve as an accompaniment to grilled or barbecued fish or chicken.

HOOTS SHOOTS SHOOTS SHOOTS SHOOTS SHOOTS

potatoes

Potatoes are one of the simplest of crops to grow. You can even grow them in large containers if they are deep enough – a plastic dustbin would be ideal provided you drill some holes in the base for drainage. They are classified either as early or maincrop. The earlies, planted in late winter to early spring, produce a crop in early summer, while you can be eating maincrops, planted a few weeks later, until well into autumn.

Get earlies off to a good start by keeping the tubers indoors, in a cool but light place and turning them periodically. This encourages them to shoot. After about 6 weeks, when the shoots will be about 2.5 cm (1 inch) long or more, plant them out in rows, about 12 cm (5 inches) deep. When the shoots are about 15 cm (6 inches) high, mound up the soil around them. This prevents the potatoes from turning green.

Potatoes are not hardy and will only take a few degrees of frost. Cover the top-growth with horticultural fleece if the nights turn cold. Start digging them up when the plants come into flower. You can leave maincrops in the ground for longer than the earlies.

Soil: Nearly all soils are suitable, provided they are enriched with garden compost or manure prior to planting.
Water: Water tubers when the size of marbles.
Conditions: Open and sunny, but sheltered from frost and strong winds.
Harvest: When the plants are in flower.
Other: Potatoes should not be grown in the same soil every year. Tomato-like fruits that sometimes appear after flowering are poisonous.

Corn and Potato Chowder

Preparation: 10 minutes
Cooking: about 1 hour 10 minutes
Serves: 4–6

2 tablespoons olive oil
1 small onion, peeled and finely chopped
2 garlic cloves, peeled and finely chopped
2 potatoes, peeled and finely chopped
900 ml (1 1/2 pints) hot vegetable stock
250 g (9 oz) smoked cod, cut into large chunks
1 x 220 g (8 oz) can sweetcorn, drained
150 ml (5 fl oz) double cream
salt and freshly ground black pepper
25 g (1 oz) chopped parsley

Heat the olive oil in a large pan and sauté the onion, over a low heat, for 2–3 minutes, until softened. Add the garlic and potatoes to the pan and cook, stirring, for a few minutes.

Add the hot stock, season with salt and pepper and bring to the boil. Cover and simmer, over a medium heat, for about 50 minutes, or until the potatoes are very soft.

Add the fish and cook for a further 5 minutes, then add the sweetcorn and cream. Heat through, stirring, until the chowder begins to bubble. Season with more salt and pepper according to taste, divide between serving bowls and sprinkle over the chopped parsley.

Hash Browns

Preparation: 10 minutes
Cooking: about 35 minutes
Serves: 6

750 g (1 1/2 lb) medium floury potatoes (such as King Edwards
    or Maris Piper), peeled
4 tablespoons sunflower oil
15 g (1/2 oz) butter
1 small onion, peeled and finely chopped
salt and freshly ground black pepper

Cook the potatoes in boiling, salted water for 15 minutes, then drain and finely chop.
Heat the oil and butter in a non-stick frying pan, add the onion, stir and cook, over a low
to moderate heat, until the onion begins to brown.

Remove the onion and add to the potatoes, season and mix well.

Shape the mixture into about 6 flat cakes. Cook the hash browns in the frying pan,
over a moderate heat, for about 15 minutes, until golden brown and crisp underneath,
adding a little more butter if the pan is dry. Turn the cakes over and lightly brown
the other side. Serve hot as part of a traditional cooked breakfast, or as an
accompaniment to a main meal.

Clam, Potato and Bean Stew

Preparation: 15 minutes
Cooking: 40 minutes
Serves: 6

2 tablespoons olive oil
125 g (4 oz) piece of pancetta, diced
1 onion, peeled and chopped
375 g (12^1/$_2$ oz) potatoes, cubed
1 leek, washed, trimmed and sliced
2 garlic cloves, peeled and crushed
1 tablespoon chopped rosemary
2 bay leaves
400 g (13 oz) can cannellini beans, drained
900 ml (1 ^{1}/$_2$ pints) vegetable stock
1 kg (2 lb) small clams or mussels, scrubbed
salt and freshly ground black pepper

For the herb oil:
150 ml (5 fl oz) extra virgin olive oil
2 large garlic cloves, peeled and sliced
^{1}/$_4$ teaspoon salt
1 tablespoon chopped parsley

Heat the oil in a large saucepan and fry the pancetta for 2–3 minutes.

Remove the pancetta and cook the onion, potatoes, leek, garlic, rosemary and bay leaves in the pan for 10 minutes. Add the beans and the stock and bring to the boil, simmering gently for 20 minutes.

For the herb oil, heat the garlic and salt in the oil and simmer for 3 minutes. Remove from the heat, cool and stir in the parsley.

Next, transfer half the soup to a blender and process until smooth. Pour it back into the pan and season with salt and pepper. Stir in the clams or mussels and add the pancetta. Simmer gently for 5 minutes when all the shellfish should be open. If some remain closed they should be discarded. Serve the soup with herb oil drizzled over and crusty bread.

leaves

heavenly herbs

oregano and marjoram

Marjoram and oregano are related hardy herbs that are widely used in Mediterranean cooking. You can harvest leaves any time the plants are in active growth from spring to autumn. They die back completely in winter. Sweet marjoram is milder in flavour than the ordinary oregano, and the plant is less hardy.

They are easy to grow either in the garden or in small pots on a kitchen window sill – probably best for sweet marjoram. Little maintenance is required beyond trimming back old straggly plants or dry twigs in spring as new growth is just beginning to appear. You can divide plants in spring or autumn for propogating new plants and keeping compact.

Soil: Poor to moderately fertile, well-drained.
Water: Keep the soil moist when in active growth.
Climate: Full sun, sheltered from wind. Sweet marjoram needs protection from frost.
Harvest: When needed, between spring and autumn.

Raspberry Pork Loins with Marjoram Courgettes

Preparation: 5 minutes
Cooking: 40–45 minutes
Serves 2

2 pork loin steaks 150g (5 oz) each
2 tablespoons olive oil
1 tablespoon honey
150g (5 oz) raspberries
2 tablespoons fresh ginger
4 medium courgettes, sliced
handful of marjoram
salt and frehly ground black pepper

Preheat the oven to 200°C, (400°F), Gas Mark 6.
    Season the pork loins with salt and pepper, then drizzle the honey over the meat.
    Oil the bottom of a roasting dish and place the meat in the dish, piling the
raspberries and fresh ginger on top.
    Cook for 40–45 minutes turning once half way through cooking. The pork will be
nicely coated with gravy and will cook in the juices from the raspberries.
    Steam the courgettes in a little water for 3 minutes or until just tender. Drain and
remove to serving plates. Sprinkle over the fresh marjoram. Add the pork drizzled with
the raspberry juices and serve.

Sicilian Risotto

Preparation: 15 minutes
Cooking: about 30 minutes
Serves: 4

3 tablespoons extra virgin olive oil
4 garlic cloves, peeled and finely chopped
1 dried red chilli, deseeded and finely chopped
4 anchovies, rinsed, dried and chopped
2 teaspoons oregano
1 tablespoon salted capers
300 g (10 oz) Arborio rice
1 glass dry white wine
2 tablespoons green olives, pitted and chopped
1.5 litres (2^1/2 pints) hot chicken or vegetable stock
2 tablespoons sun-dried tomato paste
5 or 6 sun-dried tomatoes
3 tablespoons freshly grated Parmesan cheese
salt and freshly ground black pepper

Heat the olive oil in a large pan, add the garlic, chilli, anchovies, oregano and capers
and fry for 3–4 minutes. Add the rice and cook over a high heat for 5 minutes, stirring
constantly, to coat the rice with the oil.

Add the wine and olives to the pan and simmer for 1 minute, then add 2 ladlefuls
of the stock, stir and cook for about 10 minutes, or until the liquid has been mostly
absorbed. Lower the heat and continue to cook, adding the stock, a ladle at a time,
and stirring, until the rice has absorbed the liquid. This will take about 15–20 minutes.

Stir through the sun-dried tomato paste, sun-dried tomatoes and Parmesan, and a
little more stock, if the risotto is too thick. Season with salt and pepper and allow to
stand for 5 minutes before serving.

rosemary

Rosemary is a shrubby herb from the Mediterranean. There are lots of varieties –
most are straggly bushes, some are more upright while others grow along the
ground. You can keep all of them neat by clipping them over from time to time.

The long narrow leaves are the aromatic part used to impart a delicious flavour to
cooking. Either strip them off or use lengths of stem to infuse your cooking. Try putting
a few woody stems onto the barbecue while cooking to give a subtle flavour to meat,
vegetables and fish. Either buy small plants from the garden centre for growing on or
take cuttings 15 cm long (6 inches) from established plants in summer.

Soil: Light, well-drained.
Water: Newly propagated plants and in very dry periods.
Climate: Sunny but protected from cold winter winds.
Harvest: When needed, but the flavour of leaves is best on the young stems.

Salmon Kebabs with Lime and Rosemary

Preparation: 15 minutes, plus marinating
Cooking: about 5 minutes
Serves: 3

3 salmon fillets, approximately 150–175 g (5–6 oz) each, skinned

For the marinade:
2 garlic cloves, peeled and finely chopped
4 rosemary sprigs, 1 finely chopped
100 ml ($3^1/2$ fl oz) olive oil
juice of $^1/2$ lime
2 teaspoons caster sugar
salt and freshly ground black pepper

Soak 4 wooden skewers in cold water for about 15 minutes. Rinse the salmon and pat dry, then cut into 2.5 cm (1 inch) cubes.

Thread the salmon onto the skewers and place them in a shallow heatproof dish with the whole sprigs of rosemary. Season with salt and pepper.

In a saucepan, mix together the garlic, chopped rosemary, olive oil and lime juice. Warm through, adding the sugar, and stir to combine. Remove from the heat and pour half the marinade over the fish, turning the skewers until they are well coated. Cover and leave the fish to marinate for 10 minutes.

Cook the kebabs under a hot grill, for about 5 minutes, or until cooked through, turning once during cooking. Meanwhile reheat the remaining marinade.

Transfer the kebabs to warmed serving plates and spoon over the hot marinade. Garnish with lime wedges and the hot rosemary sprigs and serve immediately with new potatoes or some steamed rice.

Florentine Steak

Preparation: 10 minutes, plus 24 hours marinating
Cooking: 10–15 minutes
Serves: 2

2 sirloin or rump steaks, approximately 400 g (13 oz) each
10 tablespoons extra virgin olive oil
5–6 rosemary sprigs
3 garlic cloves, peeled and crushed
3 handfuls of rocket
12 cherry tomatoes
2 tablespoons balsamic vinegar
salt and freshly ground black pepper

Place the steaks in a shallow, ovenproof dish. In a small bowl, mix 8 tablespoons of the olive oil with the rosemary and garlic, and season with salt and pepper. Pour this over the steaks and set aside in the fridge to marinate for 24 hours.

Grill the steaks, under a hot grill, according to taste (about 10 minutes for medium-cooked). Turn the steaks over once during cooking.

Divide the rocket leaves and cherry tomatoes between two serving plates, top with the steaks and drizzle over the balsamic vinegar and remaining 2 tablespoons of olive oil. Season with salt and pepper to taste and serve immediately. Accompany with creamy mash and minty peas or chunky chips.

Rosemary Chicken

Preparation: 20 minutes
Cooking: 20–25 minutes
Serves: 4

2 x 625 g (1 1/2 lb) oven-ready corn-fed chickens
6 tablespoons olive oil
juice of 1/2 lemon
4 tablespoons chopped rosemary leaves
salt and freshly ground black pepper

Open up the chickens along the breast bone and flatten them out onto a chopping board, using some force to push hard down so they are as flat as possible.

Rub the chickens all over, inside and out, with the olive oil, then season with salt and pepper. Drizzle the lemon juice over the skin and sprinkle the rosemary leaves onto the flesh.

Cook under a hot grill for about 15 minutes, before turning and browning the other side for a further 10 minutes. Remove from the grill, joint the chickens and serve immediately with new potatoes and steamed green beans.

sage

Sage is a wonderful Mediterranean woody evergreen plant that lives happily in borders and herb gardens. Like rosemary, it likes free-draining, even poor soil in full sun. Besides the ordinary variety with grey-green leaves, look for purple and variegated forms. Use the leaves fresh in meat dishes or dry them in a warm kitchen for crumbling into stews.

To propagate it is best to take cuttings in early autumn or in spring. In the garden, keep plants neat by clipping them over from time to time. If they become straggly and bare at the base – as they inevitably will after a few years – raise some replacements from cuttings taken in late summer.

Soil: Well-drained, preferably gravelly and not too fertile.
Water: If planting outside, give a helping hand in dry conditions.
Conditions: Full sun.
Other: Watch out for strong winds, which can break the dry older growth.

Chicken with Sage and Lemon

Preparation: 15 minutes
Cooking: 25–30 minutes
Serves: 4

4 skinless, boneless chicken breasts
2 tablespoons olive oil
2 tablespoons chopped sage
rind and juice of 2 lemons
4 sage sprigs
salt and freshly ground black pepper

Cut 4 pieces of foil, each about 30 cm (12 inches) square. Place a chicken breast in the centre of each square, season with salt and pepper and sprinkle over the chopped sage and lemon rind. Drizzle with a little lemon juice and olive oil and wrap the foil around the chicken, folding over the edges to seal.

Place the chicken parcels on a baking sheet and cook in a preheated oven, 200ºC (400ºF), Gas Mark 6, for 25 minutes. To test if cooked, unwrap a parcel and pierce the flesh with a skewer. If the juices run clear, it is cooked, if not, return to the oven for a further 5 minutes.

When cooked, place the chicken on warmed serving plates. Spoon over the juices and serve immediately with the sage sprigs and accompanied by steamed green vegetables.

Sage Butter Calves' Liver on a Leafy Bed

Preparation: 5 minutes
Cooking: about 8 minutes
Serves: 4

200 g (7 oz) baby spinach leaves
100 g (3^1/$_2$ oz) rocket
100g (3^1/$_2$ oz) watercress
100g (3^1/$_2$ oz) baby spinach
3 tablespoons extra virgin olive oil
500 g (1 lb) calves' liver
50 g (2 oz) unsalted butter
4 teaspoons chopped sage
salt and freshly ground black pepper

Place the leaves in a large serving bowl and drizzle over 1 tablespoon of the olive oil, tossing gently to combine. Divide the leaves between 4 plates.

In a frying pan, heat the remaining 2 tablespoons of olive oil over a high heat, for 2 minutes, then add the liver. Season with salt and pepper and fry the liver for 2–3 minutes. Turn the liver over and brown the other sides for a further 3 minutes, then turn once more if needed, to brown the other side. Remove the liver to the bed of salad leaves on each plate.

Place the butter in the hot frying pan and add the sage. Once the butter has melted, drizzle over the calves' liver and serve.

Sage Welsh Rarebit

Preparation: 5 minutes
Cooking: 15 minutes
Serves: 4

4 thick slices farmhouse-style bread
25g (1 oz) butter
50 g (2 oz) flour
100 ml (3^1/$_2$ fl oz) milk
250 g (9 oz) strongest mature Cheddar cheese
I tablespoon chopped fresh sage
^{1}/$_2$ red onion, finely chopped
1 teaspoon mustard powder
1 tablespoon Worcestershire sauce
pinch paprika
salt and freshly ground pepper

Toast the slices of bread under the grill on a low heat, turning them over so they are lightly browned on each side.

Now melt the butter in a small saucepan over a low heat, add the flour and heat for 2 minutes, stirring constantly. Add a little milk, mixing quickly to break up any lumps. Heat for 2 minutes and add the rest of the milk, stirring continuously. Add the chopped onion and allow the sauce to simmer for 5 minutes, stirring while it thickens.

Add the remaning ingredients and season generously, before removing from the heat and stirring to ensure the cheese has melted.

Spread thinly over the toasted bread, making sure the mixture reaches the edges and place under a hot grill for 5 minutes, or until bubbling and browned.

Sage Meatballs

Preparation: 20 minutes
Cooking: 20–25 minutes
Serves: 4

50 g (2 oz) breadcrumbs
600 ml (1 pint) milk
450 g (15^1/$_2$ oz) ground minced beef
250 g (9 oz) ground chicken
10 peeled garlic cloves, 6 crushed and 4 finely chopped
5 eggs, beaten
100 g (3^1/$_2$ oz) butter
1 vegetable stock cube
2 teaspoons dry sage
1 teaspoon grated nutmeg
handful of flat leaf parsley
salt and freshly ground black pepper

Warm 100 ml (3^1/$_2$ fl oz) of the milk in a small pan. Transfer to a bowl, add the breadcrumbs and set aside to soak. In a separate bowl, mix together the minced beef, chicken and crushed garlic, and season with salt and pepper. Add the soaked bread-crumbs and eggs to the bowl, roll together, then form the mixture into balls of roughly equal size.

In a frying pan, melt the butter then add the stock cube, chopped garlic, sage and nutmeg. Stir to combine and cook over a high heat, until the butter is golden brown. Add the remaining milk and the parsley to the pan then, when the sauce is hot, carefully drop in the meatballs.

Cook gently for 10–15 minutes, then remove a meatball, slicing to check if it is browned all the way through. Remove the meatballs from the pan with a slotted spoon and serve with boiled rice or crusty bread.

basil and mint

Basil is one of the most fragrant of culinary herbs, with a tangy sweetness that blends perfectly with tomatoes – and it is, of course, an essential ingredient of pesto. It's a half-hardy annual, so you need to grow new plants from seed each spring. Either keep the plants growing in pots on the kitchen window sill, or plant them in the garden, when all danger of frosts has passed. Basil is often sold growing in pots, but for better cropping plants raise your own from seed. Fill trays or pots with compost and sow the seed on the surface. Prick out (separate) the seedlings and, when they are large enough to handle, either pot them individually or plant them in the garden. Keep picking the leaves to keep the plants fresh, compact and productive.

Growing from seed: Indoors in spring.
Soil: Fertile and well-drained.
Conditions: Sheltered site in sun.
Water: Only in prolonged dry spells.
Harvest: When the leaves are nice and big.
Other: Basil is said to grow well near tomatoes and repels certain insect pests.

Mint prefers moist soil in a lightly shaded position. To contain its spread, grow it in a container sunk in the ground to keep the roots cool. Mint sauce is an essential accompaniment to roast lamb and is also a frequent ingredient of North African dishes and cooling yogurt dips to serve with curries. You can divide and place root cuttings in water on a kitchen window sill any time the plant is in growth, or outside in winter when the plant has died back. Take stem cuttings in spring or autumn. Growing from seed is not advised. Small plants can be kept in growth indoors over winter so you need never be without a few leaves to perk up a winter salad.

Soil: Fertile soil.
Conditions: Shade.
Water: Keep the roots moist.
Harvest: Any time the plant is in growth.

Hot Basil Salmon Steaks

Preparation: 15 minutes
Cooking: 25 minutes
Serves: 6

1 large bunch basil
4 celery stalks, chopped
1 carrot, chopped
1 small courgette, chopped
1 small onion, chopped
6 salmon steaks, about 125 g (4 oz) each
1/2 cup dry white wine
1/2 cup water
1 teaspoon lemon juice
1 tablespoon unsalted butter
salt and freshly ground pepper

Set aside a few basil leaves for garnish. Spread the chopped vegetables over the bottom of a heavy-based frying pan. Lay the salmon steaks on top, then cover with half the basil. Pour over the wine and water and season with salt and pepper.

Bring to the boil, cover, and simmer for 10 minutes. Transfer the salmon to a warmed dish. Bring the poaching liquid back to the boil and simmer for 5 minutes. Strain the liquid into a food processor, add the cooked and uncooked basil and blend to a purée then return to the saucepan. Bring the purée to the boil and reduce by half, until thickened. Remove the pan from the heat, add the lemon juice and stir in the butter. Pour the sauce over the salmon steaks and serve sprinkled with basil leaves.

Minty Pesto Cod

Preparation: 10 minutes
Cooking: about 10 minutes
Serves: 4

For the mint pesto:
6 tablespoons chopped mint
1 tablespoon chopped parsley
1 large garlic clove, peeled and chopped
1 tablespoon grated Parmesan cheese
1 tablespoon single cream
1 teaspoon balsamic vinegar
3 tablespoons extra virgin olive oil

4 cod fillets, approximately 175 g (6 oz) each
olive oil, for basting
1 tablespoon lemon juice
200 g (7 oz) green beans
salt and freshly ground black pepper

First, make the mint pesto. Place all the pesto ingredients in a blender or food processor and purée until fairly smooth.

Brush the cod steaks with olive oil and squeeze over a little lemon juice. Season with salt and pepper and cook under a hot grill for 3–4 minutes on each side, until just coloured.

Meanwhile, bring a little water to the boil in a pan, add the beans, cover and steam for 4–5 minutes. Drain the beans.

To serve, make a small pile of beans, lay the cod fillets on top and add a large spoonful of pesto on top of each piece of fish.

dill

It's the feathery, aniseed-tasting foliage that makes dill so valuable for cooking, so it's best to start cutting leafy stalks off the plant before the flower heads appear in summer. It seems to have a particular affinity with fish.

Dill is an annual that's more or less hardy, though it's probably best to start seed off under cover for early plants. Sow in modules, as the plants don't like too much disturbance. You can also sow dill *in situ* in early summer. The leaves, if you can spare any, are also good fillers in flower arrangements, and the whole plant is attractive when grown in borders. You can use fresh dill or dry the frond-like leaves on a wire rack in a shady, cool but dry place. Crumble the leaves when dry and store them in a screw-top jar.

Growing from seed: Spring to summer.
Soil: Fertile and well drained. Dill bolts (runs to seed) in poor soil, and the flavour will suffer as a result.
Conditions: Full sun with protection from strong winds.
Water: Water seedlings and in dry periods or it will bolt (see above).
Harvest: Keep cutting leaves to stimulate further leaf production.
Other: Cabbage plants like to grow near dill as do lettuce and cucumber.

LEAVES LEAVES LEAVES LEAVES LEAVES LEAVES LEAVE

Cucumber and Dill Soup

Serves: 4
Preparation time: 20 minutes, plus cooling and chilling time
Cooking time: 40 minutes

$1^1/_2$ large cucumbers
1 small handful of fresh mint
1 small handful of fresh dill
500 ml (16 fl oz) cold chicken or vegetable stock
150 ml (5 fl oz) natural yogurt
4 tablespoons natural yogurt, to serve
fresh dill and/or mint sprigs
salt and freshly ground black pepper

Trim the ends off the cucumber and discard, then chop the cucumber into chunks and blend in a food processor. Add most of the mint and the dill, reserving a little for the garnish. Process some more, then add the stock and process again until well mixed.

Strain the soup through a fine sieve, then return to the blender, adding in the yogurt and mixing until evenly blended. Season to taste with salt and pepper.

Cover and refrigerate for at least 4 hours. Whisk the soup well before serving and season to taste. Pour into individual soup bowls, swirling a spoonful of yogurt into the centre of each bowl. Garnish with the reserved mint and dill leaves. Serve chilled with wafer thin pieces of crispbread.

bay

Bay is an evergreen tree that can be kept as a dwarf shrub with regular clipping. You can grow it as a free-standing plant or in containers. Bay is often pruned into shapes such as pyramids, cones, balls or standards and it makes a lovely aromatic hedge in mild climates.

The handsome, dull green leaves are not actually edible, but are usually cut in half – fresh or dry – to impart flavour to a variety of dishes. To dry leaves, cut stems in summer and hang them in a warm kitchen. Store the dried leaves in a screw-top jar. If you have an open fire, throw some stems onto the flames in winter for a companionable crackle and delicious scent. You can propagate bay from stem cuttings in late summer.

Soil: Fertile, free-draining.
Water: Keep well watered when establishing itself.
Conditions: Full sun and must be protected from harsh cold winds.
Harvest: Cut off individual leaves.
Other: Prune out areas damaged by frost or cold winds.

Bouillabaisse

Preparation: 20 minutes
Cooking: 30–35 minutes
Serves: 4

1/2 chicken stock cube
12 new potatoes
3 tablespoons olive oil
1 small fennel bulb, core removed and finely sliced
1 onion, peeled and finely chopped
3 garlic cloves, peeled and finely chopped
1/2 teaspoon fennel seeds
handful of flat leaf parsley, chopped,
1 bay leaf
4 plum tomatoes, skins removed and chopped
2 strips orange rind, approximately 1 x 7 cm (1/2 x 3 inches) long
pinch of saffron
400 g (13 oz) cod, haddock or other firm, white fish, sliced into 2.5 cm
    (1 inch) chunks
200 g (7 oz) raw or cooked king prawns
1 teaspoon chopped thyme
salt and freshly ground black pepper

Make up the chicken stock, using the stock cube, with 0.5 litres (1 pint) water and leave to simmer.

Bring a large pan of boiling, salted water to the boil, add the potatoes and cook for about 10 minutes, until par-boiled. Drain the potatoes, return to the pan, cover with cold water then, after a minute or two, remove the skins.

Heat the olive oil in a large pan, add the fennel, onion and garlic and fry for 5 minutes until browned. Add the fennel seeds, most of the parsley, bay leaf, and season with salt and pepper. Cook for 5 minutes then add the tomatoes, orange rind, thyme and extra seasoning and cook for a further 6–7 minutes. Stir the saffron into the stock and pour this over the vegetables.

Add the fish to the pan, then the potatoes and prawns, and heat through, until the fish is cooked. Remove the bay leaf, garnish with parsley and serve.

thyme

Thyme is a low-growing, evergreen herb, ideal for growing in the gaps between paving slabs. Tough and hardy, it takes a certain amount of wear and tear, releasing a delicious aroma when bruised by gentle footfall. There is a large number of varieties, some with an almost citrus scent.

Buy small plants from a herb nursery, if you can. They do well in a rock garden, or anywhere where the soil is free-draining. If you want to grow thyme in pots, cover the compost surface with a layer of grit. Clip plants over after flowering to keep them neat. If you want more plants, simply pull them apart in spring or autumn. Gather the leaves as and when you need them.

Soil: Light, even poor, and well-drained.
Water: In dry conditions, or when in a small container which will dry out quickly.
Conditions: Full sun.
Harvest: As needed.

Thyme Roasted Root Vegetables

Preparation: 15 minutes
Cooking: about 40 minutes
Serves: 4

2 tablespoons olive oil
3 carrots, thickly cut
2 parsnips, thickly cut
2 turnips, thickly cut
1 fennel bulb, thickly cut
4 garlic cloves, peeled and chopped
3 thyme sprigs
1 1/2 tablespoons honey
125 ml (4 fl oz) white wine
salt and freshly ground black pepper

Preheat the oven to 200ºC (400ºF), Gas Mark 6. Heat the olive oil in a large frying pan, add all the vegetables and the garlic and fry until slightly browned. Add the thyme, honey and white wine, season with salt and pepper and stir.

Transfer the vegetables to an ovenproof dish and place in the preheated oven for 25 minutes, stirring and basting occasionally. Remove and serve with steamed couscous or as an accompaniment to roast meat.

Green Herb Risotto

Preparation: 10 minutes
Cooking: about 30 minutes
Serves: 4

900 ml (1 1/2 pints) chicken or vegetable stock
2 tablespoons butter
1 tablespoon olive oil
1 onion, peeled and finely chopped
1 garlic clove, peeled and chopped
200 g (7 oz) Arborio rice
handful each of parsley, basil, oregano and thyme, chopped
75 g (3 oz) grated Parmesan cheese
salt and freshly ground black pepper
sage sprigs, to garnish

Heat the stock in a large pan until it starts to simmer.

In a separate pan, melt the butter, then add the olive oil, onion and garlic and sauté for 3 minutes. Add the rice to the pan, stirring well to coat the grains all over, then add 2 ladlefuls of hot stock to cover the rice. Cook, stirring, until all the liquid has been absorbed. Continue to add the stock, a ladle at a time, and cook, stirring, until it has all been absorbed and the rice is coated in a creamy sauce. This will take about 15–20 minutes.

Add the herbs and Parmesan to the pan, season with salt and pepper and stir well. Cover and set aside for a couple of minutes, until the cheese has melted. Serve garnished with sage sprigs.

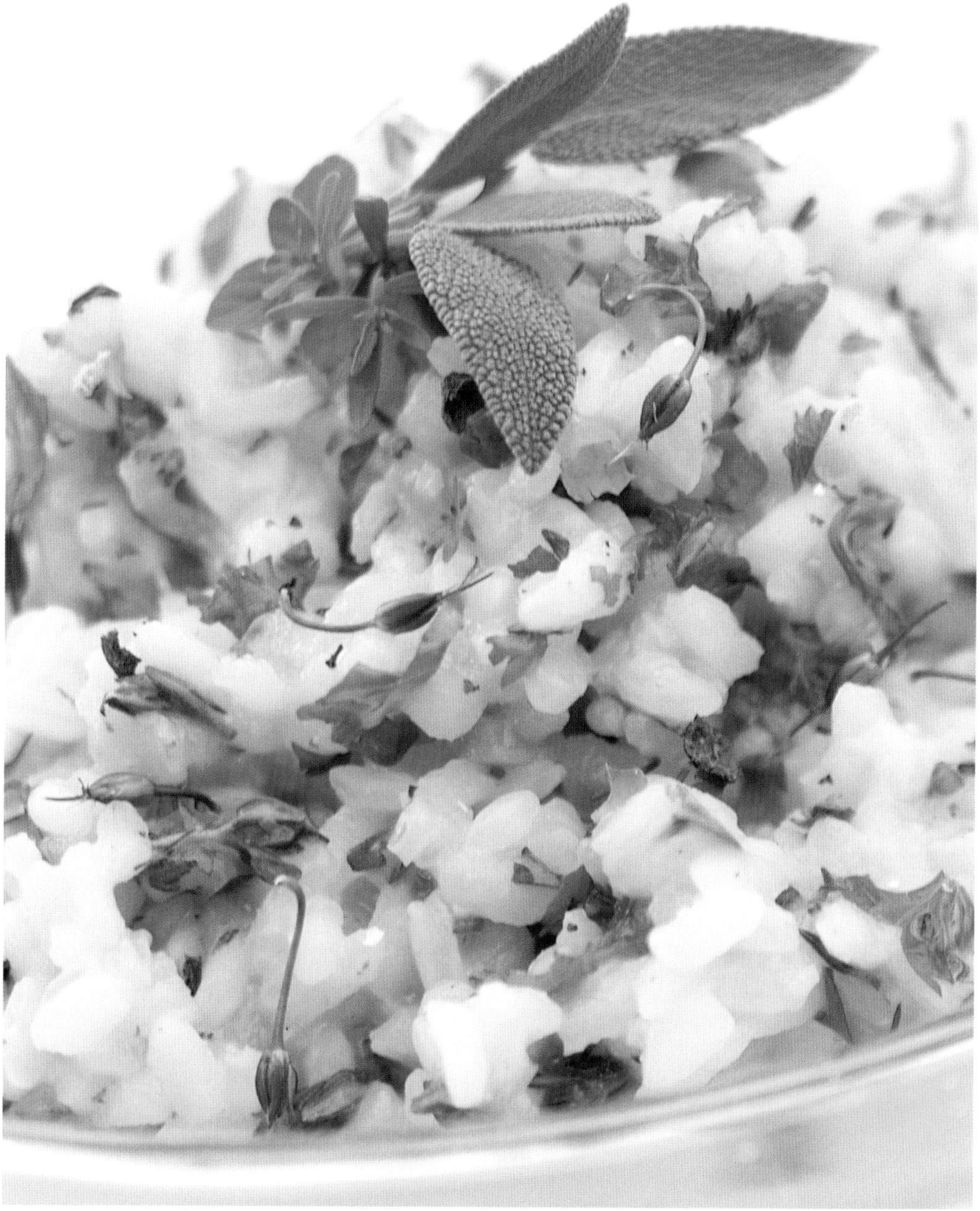

chives

Chives are related to onions, and it's the leaves that are used to impart a mild but distinctive onion flavour to almost any savoury dish – such as pasta, soups or salads. In the garden, they are a pretty plant that come up year after year, useful as an edging to a border, with appealing purplish pink flowers in summer that are also edible. Chives can also be grown in containers and you can divide clumps in spring or autumn to propagate.

Chives are actually bulbs, and are usually sold as growing plants, ready for planting out. The plants die back in winter, but if you want early leaves you can dig up a small number of dormant bulbs in late winter, pot them up and bring them into the gentle warmth of the kitchen. They will produce a sheaf of fresh leaves for cutting before your garden plants.

Growing from seed: *In situ* in spring.
Soil: Moist, well-drained soil.
Water: Do not over-water.
Conditions: Sun or light shade.
Harvest: When needed, when the plants are in growth.
Other: Cut flower stalks off after blooming to produce more leaves.

Chive, Red Pepper and Goat's Cheese Frittata

Preparation: 12 minutes
Cooking: 15 minutes
Serves: 4–6

250 g (9 oz) new potatoes, cut into chunks
2 tablespoons olive oil
2 red peppers, deseeded and cut into chunks
7 eggs
4 tablespoons milk
2 tablespoons snipped chives, plus extra to garnish
1 goat's cheese log, sliced into 6 rounds
salt and freshly ground black pepper

Place the new potatoes in a saucepan of cold, salted water and bring to the boil.
Cook for 7 minutes, or until just cooked through but not soggy. Drain and set aside.

Heat the oil in a large, heavy-based frying pan. Add the potatoes and peppers and fry over a medium heat for about 5 minutes, until the peppers have softened and the potato has turned golden brown. Remove the pan from the heat.

In a large bowl combine the eggs, milk, chives and salt and pepper. Whisk together for about 1 minute until the egg mixture is frothy. Return the frying pan to the heat and pour in the egg mixture. As the frittata begins to set, loosen the edges with a spatula. Cover with a lid and cook for about 7 minutes, until the egg mixture is almost set, then remove from the heat and arrange the cheese slices on top.

Place the frying pan under a medium grill for 5 minutes until the top of the frittata is set and golden brown and the cheese is just starting to melt.

Remove from the grill, loosen the edges of the frittata with a knife or spatula and holding a plate over the frying pan turn out the frittata, turning it back onto a second plate so that it is golden side up. Slice into wedges and serve with a sprinkling of chives, crusty bread and a green salad.

Ricotta and Chive Bread

Preparation: 20 minutes, plus resting
Cooking: 25 minutes
Serves: 6

500 g (1 lb) strong white flour, plus extra for sprinkling
1 1/2 teaspoons salt
25 g (1 oz) yeast
75 ml (3 fl oz) olive oil
300 ml (1/2 pint) water
125 g (4 oz) ricotta or cream cheese
2 tablespoons snipped chives

In a large bowl, mix together the flour, salt, yeast, olive oil, water and cheese, using your hands. Remove and place on a lightly floured surface, then knead for 2 minutes. Add the chives and knead for a further 3 minutes, then return the dough to the bowl and set aside to rest for 1 hour.

Line a baking tray with baking paper. Tip the dough out onto a lightly floured surface and mould into a sausage shape that is tapered at each end. Place the bread on the baking tray and set aside to rise, for 1 hour. Preheat the oven to 220°C (425°F), Gas Mark 7. Bake the bread for 25 minutes. When cooked, transfer to a wire rack to cool.

parsley and coriander

Best treated as an annual, parsley can – and often does – survive the winter. Cut off any flower stems that appear as flowering ruins the flavour. There are flat-leaved and curly varieties, with slighly variable flavours. Pots of growing parsley are widely available to grow on the window sill. You can speed up germination by soaking the seed over-night in hot water before sowing. Otherwise, allow up to 6 weeks for the first seedlings to appear. Grow the small plants on in pots and you can plant them out in the garden once all danger of frost has passed. They make a delightful edging to a vegetable plot, or indeed to more ornamental planting, and plants are said to deter certain insect pests.

Growing from seed: Seed can be sown from spring to summer.
Soil: Fertile, well-drained.
Conditions: Sun or light shade.
Water: Only in very dry periods.
Harvest: Spring to autumn; also through winter if plants survive.
Other: Keep cutting the leaves to ensure a continuous supply.

Coriander is a wonderful cooling annual herb that is an essential part of many curries. Both the leaves and seeds can be used in cooking, but note that some varieties have been specifically bred for leaf production, while others are better seed-setters. If you want seeds, aim to sow late winter, for maximum growing period. Coriander for seed is also best grown in a hot, sunny position, while leaf varieties are best in light shade. Keep picking the leaves to prevent the plants from flowering, after which the flavour coarsens.

Growing from seed: Sow seed from spring to summer.
Soil: Fertile, well-drained soil is best.
Conditions: Sun (for seed) or light shade (for leaves).
Water: Keep the young plants well watered or they may bolt.
Harvest: Cut leaves throughout the growing period. For seed, cut stems from the plants in late summer/autumn and hang upside down in a paper bag in a warm kitchen.

Mediterranean Kebabs

Preparation: 15 minutes, plus 1½ hours marinating
Cooking: 8–10 minutes
Serves: 4–6

250 g (9 oz) haloumi cheese, cubed
2 courgettes, trimmed and thickly sliced
1 red and 1 yellow pepper, deseeded and cut
    into 2.5 cm (1 inch) squares
175 g (6 oz) cherry tomatoes
1 red onion, peeled and cut into chunks
100g (3½ oz) button mushrooms

For the marinade:
1 garlic clove, peeled and crushed
handful of fresh coriander, chopped
4 tablespoons olive oil
1 tablespoon lemon juice
salt and freshly ground black pepper

Soak 6 wooden skewers in water while preparing the ingredients. Thread the haloumi, courgette slices, pepper, cherry tomatoes, onion and mushrooms onto the skewers.

In a small bowl, mix together all the ingredients for the marinade. Arrange the kebabs in a row on the base of a heatproof dish and pour over the marinade. Set aside for 1½ hours, turning and spooning over the marinade occasionally.

Cook under a hot grill, for about 8–10 minutes, turning occasionally, until lightly charred at the edges. Brush the kebabs with any remaining marinade before serving, with steamed couscous or Turkish bread, and a green salad.

If weather permits, these kebabs can easily be cooked on the barbecue.

eats

fruity sweets

strawberries and raspberries

Strawberries are incredibly easy to grow, either in the garden or in special containers that have pockets for each plant. Buy small plants in spring, or in late summer to early autumn for crops the following summer. Tiny alpine strawberries are particularly delicious.

Improve the soil first with rotted manure or compost, then plant the strawberries 35 cm (14 inches) apart. Keep them well watered in dry spells. You may need to protect the fruits from mice and birds, using nets.

Soil: Fertile, well-drained.
Climate: Warm and sunny spot. Alpine strawberries tolerate shade.
Water: Water regularly, especially when in flower and fruit.
Harvest: When the fruits are ripe.
Other: Remove damaged and/or rotten fruits that will attract pests. Replace plants every 3 to 4 years

Depending on the variety, raspberries fruit in summer or autumn. You usually buy them as leafless canes in winter. Improve the soil with manure or compost before planting. The best way to grow them is tied to horizontal wires stretched between two uprights.

Prune summer raspberries immediately after you have eaten the crop. Cut the old stems down to the base, then tie in the new shoots to the support – these will produce fruit next year. Autumn raspberries are even easier. Just cut back all the stems in late winter.

Soil: Fertile, well-drained.
Climate: Sheltered and sunny spot. They tolerate some shade.
Water: Water regularly during dry spells.
Harvest: When the fruits are ripe.
Other: Fork well-rotted manure around the canes every spring.

Strawberry Pavlova

Preparation: 20 minutes
Cooking: 1 hour
Serves: 6

3 large egg whites (at room temperature)
175 g (6 oz) caster sugar
1/2 teaspoon white wine vinegar
1 teaspoon cornflour
300 ml (1/2 pint) double or whipping cream
250 g (9 oz) strawberries, hulled and sliced
1 kiwi fruit, peeled and sliced

Preheat the oven to 160°C (325°F), Gas Mark 3. Draw a 25 cm (10 inch) circle in the centre of a sheet of baking paper. Turn the paper upside down on a baking sheet and oil lightly.

In a large, grease-free bowl, whisk the egg whites until they form soft peaks. Now start to whisk in the caster sugar a little at a time. Continue whisking until the mixture is stiff and glossy, then whisk in the white wine vinegar and cornflour.

Using a metal spoon, spread the meringue mixture onto the paper about 5 mm (1/4 inch) inside the circle (the meringue will spread out slightly). Use the spoon to create swirled, slightly raised edges and a lower centre.

Bake in the preheated oven for 1 hour, until the outside is dry and crisp and the centre is cooked. Turn off the heat and allow to cool in the oven.

Loosen the meringue with a palette knife and transfer to a plate. Whip the cream and pile it into the hollow of the meringue. Top with the strawberries and kiwi fruit.

Knickerbocker Glory

Preparation: 10 minutes
Serves: 4

100 ml (3^1/$_2$ fl oz) double or whipping cream
1 tub crème caramel
500 g (1 lb) strawberries
4 apples, quartered
8 scoops of ice cream of different flavours
4 cherries

Whip the cream in a small bowl. Divide the crème caramel between four large glasses. Top with the ice cream, apples and strawberries, and finally the whipped cream and a cherry. Serve at once.

Raspberry White Chocolate Cheesecake

Preparation: 20 minutes, plus chilling
Serves: 4–6

200 g (7 oz) shortbread biscuits
50 g (2 oz) unsalted butter
300 g (10 oz) full-fat soft cream cheese
200 g (7 oz) fromage frais
200 g (7 oz) white chocolate, melted
250 g (9 oz) raspberries, chopped

Place the biscuits in a plastic bag and crush with a rolling pin, until they are broken into crumbs. Melt the butter in a saucepan over a low heat then stir in the crushed biscuits. Press this mixture into the base and sides of a 23 cm (9 inch) tin, with a removable base. Set aside in the fridge to chill, while preparing the other ingredients.

In a large bowl, beat the cream cheese and fromage frais together, then add the raspberries. Melt the chocolate in a bowl, over a pan of boiling water (or in the microwave), and add to the cheese mixture. Remove the base from the fridge, spoon in the filling and return to the fridge to chill for at least 4 hours, or overnight.

Coconut Rice Pudding with Raspberries

Preparation: 10 minutes
Cooking: 2–2$^1/_2$ hours
Serves: 6

175 g (6 oz) short-grain or round-grain pudding rice
800 ml (1$^1/_3$ pint) coconut milk
100 ml (3$^1/_2$ fl oz) milk
1 large strip of lime rind
50 g (2 oz) caster sugar
knob of butter
pinch of nutmeg
500g (1 lb) raspberries
icing sugar, to dust

Preheat the oven to 160°C (325°F), Gas Mark 3. In a large bowl, mix together the rice, coconut milk, milk, lime rind and sugar.

Pour the mixture into a lightly greased ovenproof dish. Sprinkle over the nutmeg and bake in the preheated oven for 1 hour, stirring once after 30 minutes.

Remove from the oven, stir well and remove the lime rind, dot the surface with butter and return to the oven for a further 1–1$^1/_2$ hours. The pudding is cooked when most of the liquid has been absorbed and there is a golden brown skin on top. Serve with the raspberries, and dust with the icing sugar.

rhubarb

Though we think of it as a fruit, rhubarb is actually a vegetable, as it's the stems that are used in cooking. The rest of the plant is actually poisonous, as indeed are the stems when raw. Rhubarb stems are best harvested as young as possible, while still pink or red, certainly before they have thickened and turned green. Leave at least four stalks on the plant.

To ensure a good early crop of long pink stems, put a rhubarb forcer (or failing that an inverted plastic bin) over the crown in late winter. You can't do this every year, though, as the plant will take a full year to recover from this treatment.

Soil: Fertile, reliably moist.
Climate: Full sun.
Water: Regularly throughout the growing season.
Harvest: Late winter to early summer.

Rhubarb Fool

Preparation: 15 minutes, plus 1 hour chilling
Cooking: 10 minutes
Serves: 4–6

500 g (1 lb) rhubarb, washed and trimmed
100 g (3^1/$_2$ oz) soft brown sugar
2 tablespoons freshly grated ginger
2 bananas, thinly sliced
250 g (9 oz) quark (soft cheese)
2 egg whites, whisked into stiff peaks

Cut the rhubarb into chunks and place in a saucepan with the brown sugar and
2 tablespoons of water. Turn the heat to low and allow the rhubarb to sweat until the
juices begin to run.

Remove from the heat and purée the rhubarb in a food processor with the ginger
and most of the banana until it forms a runny mixture. Place the quark in a large mixing
bowl then gradually beat in the blended fruit mixture.

Fold in the egg whites, then transfer the mixture into individual dishes and chill in
the fridge for 1 hour. Top with the remaining banana and serve.

Rhubarb, Ginger and Almond Cake

Preparation: 15 minutes
Cooking: 30 minutes
Serves: 6–8

1 tablespoon unsalted butter, plus extra for greasing
50 g (2 oz) ground almonds
3 eggs, beaten
125 ml (4^1/$_2$ fl oz) milk
250 g (9 oz) caster sugar
1 tablespoon grated fresh ginger
250 g (9 oz) plain flour
2 teaspoons baking powder
300 g (10 oz) rhubarb, cut into 7 cm (3 inch)
    pieces

Preheat the oven to 200°C (400°F), Gas Mark 6. Grease a round 20 cm (8 inch) loose-bottomed or springform cake tin. Sprinkle in half of the ground almonds and shake them around so that they stick to the tin.

Combine the dry ingredients and ginger in a large mixing bowl. Make a well in the centre, pour in the eggs and milk and whisk to form a thick batter. Spoon the mixture into the tin, lay the rhubarb pieces on top, then sprinkle on the remaining almonds and dot with butter.

Bake in the preheated oven for 1^1/$_2$ hours, or until the top is golden and the cake is cooked through. Remove and cool. Dust with icing sugar and serve with crème fraiche or whipped cream.

apples and pears

Apples needn't be restricted to the large trees, which bear fruit that is out of reach. An apple tree in a container is a beautiful addition to a porch or patio, marking the seasons with blossom in spring and bearing apples through the summer until autumn harvest. Pruning and training your tree will increase the harvest and keep the tree compact. Prune new summer growth (with no fruit) to five or six leaves in late July, then cut back again in winter to just above the third bud. This concentrates growth in the part which bears fruit. Apples are late to flower and so are safe from frosts.

Planting: Autumn–winter.
Soil: Well-drained and fertile.
Water: Water well during early stages.
Conditions: Sunny and sheltered sites are best.
Harvest: Late summer to late winter depending on variety.
Other: Thin out the fruit to obtain good size and quality fruit.

Pears require similar conditions to apples and have few pruning requirements when very young. All that is needed is to cut out dead or diseased wood and to prune in summer aiming for one or two fruit per cluster. Two trees in pots in either side of an archway or door resolves the problem of pollination, though some varieties are self-fertile. Choose your variety carefully and make sure it is grown on a dwarfing rootstock.

Planting: Autumn.
Soil: Dislikes chalk.
Water: When establishing itself water well, then in dry periods.
Conditions: Warm and sheltered from strong winds and frost or they will not bear fruit.
Harvest: Mid-summer to mid-spring.
Other: The fruit ripens in stages so it's worth picking over the tree at intervals.

Dutch Cinnamon Apple Sauce

Preparation: 15 minutes
Cooking: 30–40 minutes
Serves: 6–8

I kg (2 lb) apples, peeled and quartered
2 teaspoons nutmeg
1 teaspoon mixed spice
1 cinnamon stick
25 g (1 oz) caster sugar, plus extra, (according to taste)

One-quarter fill a large saucepan with water and add all the ingredients to the pan. Bring to the boil and cook, covered, over a medium heat, for about 30 minutes, until the apples have softened.

Using a potato masher, push the apples down into the pan. If they are still firm, continue cooking for a further 10–15 minutes.

Remove from the heat and discard the cinnamon stick. Serve with a swirl of plain natural yogurt, a dusting of cinnamon and extra sugar, to taste.

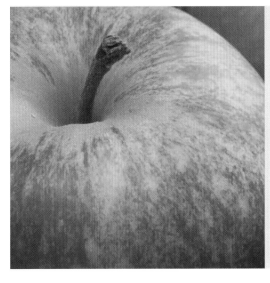

Cranberry Pears

Preparation: 20 minutes
Cooking: about 40 minutes
Serves: 4

4 large, ripe pears, peeled and stalks left intact
300 g (10 oz) cranberries, defrosted, if frozen
1 tablespoon chopped hazelnuts
3 tablespoons honey
150 ml (5 fl oz) dry white wine
few drops of red food colouring
mint sprigs, to decorate

Preheat the oven to 200ºC (400ºF), Gas Mark 6. Turn the pears upside down and, working from the base, use a small teaspoon to carefully scoop out the cores. Chop 2 tablespoons of the cranberries and mix with the hazelnuts and 1 tablespoon of the honey. Press the mixture inside the pears, using the back of a spoon.

Put the remaining cranberries, the honey, wine and a few drops of food colouring, into a flameproof and ovenproof pan. Bring to the boil, over a medium heat, and simmer for 5 minutes. Remove from the heat, place the pears upright in the pan and spoon the wine sauce over the top.

Cover the pan with foil and cook in the preheated oven, for 30 minutes, basting the pears with the sauce after 15 minutes.

Serve immediately, decorated with the mint sprigs. Alternatively, set aside in the fridge to chill, and serve cold.

cherries and plums

Cherry trees have attractive spring blossoms and sweet varieties are delicious for fruit straight off the tree. Two separate plants are needed for good pollination or one self-fertile one. Sour varieties are better for cooking, and you only need one plant. Cherry trees can grow large, but varieties grafted onto dwarfing rootstocks stay small. Train them as fans, for growing along wires, either tied to free-standing supports or strung against a wall. Prune cherries in mid-summer to remove dead or diseased wood. Trim new growth to expose ripening fruit to the sun. Leave some old wood unpruned, as this is also fruit-bearing. Birds can be a problem as they peck at buds and blossom as well as fruits, but you can net the trees to deter them.

Soil: Fertile, deep well-drained soil.
Conditions: Sheltered spot with full sun for sweet varieties; sour cherries will grow in shade. Protect the blossom from frosts.
Water: Regular watering between blossoming and fruiting.
Other: 'Stella' is a sweet variety; 'Morello' is good for cooking. These are self-pollinating – so are ideal if you only have space for one tree.

Plums are easy to grow and beautiful when the flowers open in spring. Eat the plums fresh from the tree in late summer, and they are delicious in cakes and tarts – cinnamon seems to enhance their flavour. As with cherries, it's possible to buy bush, standard or fan-trained plants ready-trained and self-fertile varieties are available if space is scarce.

Pruning plum trees can be risky, but if it is necessary, it's best to do it in summer when the weather is dry. This minimises the chances of fungal infections. Take out older and any damaged wood, and remove any branches that cross. If very full of fruit, the weight may bend some branches, causing them to split. To prevent this, thin the fruit in summer.

Soil: Fertile, well-drained.
Water: Ensure well-watered during fruiting. Less in winter.
Harvest: When fruits are soft to the touch, gently twist them off.
Conditions: Sunny and sheltered. Protect blossom from frosts in cold areas.
Other: 'Victoria' is self-fertile.

Plum Tart

Preparation: 25 minutes, plus cooling
Cooking: 30–40 minutes
Serves: 6

90 g (3¹/₂ oz) butter, plus extra for greasing
175 g (6 oz) plain flour
4 tablespoons iced water
pinch of salt
40 g (1¹/₂ oz) caster sugar, plus 4 teaspoons for pastry
1 kg (2 lb) plums, stoned and quartered
pinch of cinnamon

Lightly grease a 20 cm (8 inch) flan tin with butter and preheat the oven to 200°C (400°F), Gas Mark 6. In a large bowl, rub the butter into the flour, adding 2 tablespoons of the water, to moisten. Add the salt and 4 teaspoons sugar to the mixture, which should be crumbly, not sticky.

Form the mixture into a ball, then press the pastry into the greased tin, spreading it over the base and up the sides. Arrange the plums on the pastry in concentric circles, beginning in the centre and working outwards, overlapping the fruit as it will shrink when cooked.

Sprinkle over the sugar and cinnamon and place the tin on a baking sheet. Bake in the preheated oven for 30–40 minutes, until golden. Remove from the oven and allow to cool for 10 minutes, before transferring to a cooling rack. Serve hot or cold, with vanilla ice cream or freshly whipped cream.

Cherry Puffs

Preparation: 15 minutes
Cooking: 15 minutes
Makes: 7

1 sheet ready-rolled puff pastry
1 egg, beaten
100 ml (3¹/2 fl oz) whipped cream or crème fraîche
21 cherries

Remove the pastry from the fridge 1 hour before using. Preheat the oven to 220ºC (425 ºF), Gas mark 6. Place the pastry on a lightly floured board and cut out seven 7 cm (3 inch) rounds. Place the rounds on a greased baking tray and, using a cutter, score a smaller concentric circle within each of those circles. Be careful not to cut right through the pastry.

Brush the rim of each circle with beaten egg and bake in the preheated oven, for 15 minutes, until well risen and golden.

Remove from the oven and leave to cool on a wire rack. Cut out the lids of the smaller circles where you scored the pastry earlier (the pastry layers will have separated when cooking). Fill the holes with a little whipped cream or crème fraîche and top each one with 3 cherries. Serve at once.

peaches and nectarines

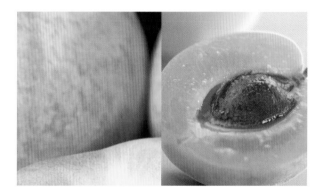

Peaches and the slightly more vulnerable nectarines need a sheltered spot in the garden. For best fruiting in a cold area, train them against a warm wall, fanning out the main branches as they grow. You may still need to protect the blossom from late frosts with horticultural fleece. Alternatively, grow them in pots and bring them under cover if the weather turns nasty. It's usually necessary to hand-pollinate the blossom with a paintbrush – a delightful job in early spring. Thinning the developing fruits will encourage the remainder to grow larger. After picking the fruit in late summer, cut back the fruited wood to a new shoot, which will flower and fruit the following year.

Soil: Fertile and well-drained.
Conditions: Warm and sunny, sheltered from frost and strong winds.
Water: Water well, especially in dry conditions.
Harvest: Late summer to early autumn.
Other: Keep the plants dry in winter by shielding them with polythene sheeting or, if they are in pots, bringing them in during wet spells. This helps prevent leaf curl.

Peaches in White Wine with Ice Cream

Preparation: 10 minutes, plus 1 hour chilling
Cooking: about 12 minutes
Serves: 4

4 peaches
4 tablespoons caster sugar
500 ml (17 fl oz) dry white wine
1 cinnamon stick
4 scoops vanilla ice cream
handful of mint leaves

Bring a large pan of water to the boil and blanch the peaches for about 2 minutes (this helps the skins peel off easily).

Peel, halve, stone and slice the peaches, sprinkle with sugar and place in a large pan. Pour over the wine, add the cinnamon and then heat, covered, for 10 minutes.

Remove the fruit to serving dishes, pour over the syrup and set aside in the fridge for 1 hour. Serve with the ice cream and a few mint sprigs.

Marsala Baked Peach Brulée

Preparation: 20 minutes, plus chilling
Cooking: 25–30 minutes
Serves: 6

2 ripe peaches, halved, stoned and thinly sliced
50 ml (2 fl oz) Marsala (or sherry)
90 g (3 oz) caster sugar, plus extra for sprinkling
8 egg yolks
350 ml (12 fl oz) double cream
150 g (5 oz) mascarpone cheese

Place the peaches in a large pan with the Marsala and half the sugar. Heat, cover, and cook for 5 minutes, then leave to cool.

Preheat the oven to 180°C (350°F), Gas Mark 4. In a large bowl, mix together the egg yolks and remaining sugar, using a fork. Pour the cream into a pan and cook over a medium heat until it starts to thicken and bubble. Remove from the heat and gradually stir the cream into the egg mixture. Drain the peaches, reserving the liquid, and set aside.

Put the mascarpone in a bowl and pour over the peach cooking liquid, then beat together well. Slowly pour the cream and egg mix, through a sieve, into the mascarpone and whisk until smooth.

Arrange 6 heatproof ramekin dishes on a heavy-based baking tray and divide the mixture evenly between them. Transfer to the oven and cook for 20–25 minutes, until set. Remove the dishes to the fridge and chill for 3–4 hours.

Remove the desserts from the fridge and arrange the peach slices on top, then sprinkle over a little caster sugar. Place the dishes under a hot grill, and cook for a few minutes, removing when the sugar starts to brown and caramelise.

redcurrants

As well as being a traditional accompaniment to game when made into jelly, redcurrants also lend a tartness to sweeter dishes. Their jewel-like berries ripen in mid-summer and, to retain their shape, need only light cooking.

You can grow them as free-standing bushes, perhaps as an informal hedge in the kitchen garden, or trained on horizontal wires, or even in containers. Prune them in winter to relieve congestion and remove the older wood. The idea is to produce a strong framework of branches. The berries are highly attractive to birds and squirrels, so you will need either to net your plants to keep them off, or grow them in a fruit cage.

Soil: Fertile and well-drained.
Water: Regularly, especially while in fruit.
Conditions: They are best in sun, but tolerate some shade.
Harvest: When ripe.
Other: 'Raby Castle' is a lovely variety, developed in 1820 and still grown today.

Strawberry and Redcurrant Millefeuille

Preparation: 10 minutes
Cooking: about 20 minutes
Serves: 4

For the coulis:
175 g (6 oz) raspberries
3 tablespoons caster sugar, plus extra (according to taste)
4 tablespoons water

1 sheet ready-rolled puff pastry
1 x 100 ml (3^1/$_2$ fl oz) carton fromage frais
200 g (7 oz) strawberries, sliced
4 small bunches of redcurrants
icing sugar, to dust

Remove the puff pastry from the fridge 1 hour before cooking. Preheat the oven to 200°C (400°F), Gas mark 6.

Heat the raspberries, sugar and water in a pan, stirring frequently, until the raspberries have disintegrated. Remove from the heat and strain the coulis through a fine sieve, discarding the seedy pulp.

Add sugar to taste, if required, then return the coulis to the pan and simmer gently for 10 minutes, until it thickens slightly.

Roll out the pastry and use a cutter or a large glass to make four 7 cm (3 inch) rounds. Place the rounds on a greased baking sheet and cook in the oven for 15 minutes, until well risen and golden.

Cut the pastry rounds in half through their middle and place one half on each serving plate. Spoon on a dollop of fromage frais, then top with some strawberries. Carefully top with another pastry round, drizzle the coulis round the millefeuille and garnish with a bunch of redcurrants. Dust each millefeuille with icing sugar. Serve at once.

grapes

Grapes are hardier than is commonly supposed, but they do need a warm, sheltered site if the fruits are to ripen fully. If you live in an area where late frosts are common, grow them in a greenhouse. They need plenty of space for the roots and vine. Grapes can be black or white and are classified as either dessert – for eating straight from the vine – or wine. A few are grown for both.

Train the vines on horizontal wires. Prune in spring to reduce the number of bunches, then again in summer to make sure the ripening berries are exposed to the sunlight. In winter, cut back all the previous season's growth to a woody framework.

Soil: Moderately fertile and well-drained. Excessively rich soil encourages leafy growth at the expense of fruits.
Conditions: Warm, sunny and sheltered on a south-facing slope if possible.
Water: Water freely during dry spells, especially when the fruits are developing.
Other: Watch out for frosts when the vine is in flower, and protect with horticultural fleece overnight, if necessary.

Caramelized Grape Ice-Cream

Preparation: 1 hour, plus 4 hours freezing
Cooking: 30 minutes
Serves: 6

1 litre (1²/₃ pints) red grape juice
4 egg yolks
250 ml (9 fl oz) double cream
200 g (7 oz) granulated sugar
4 little bunches of grapes
1 egg white, lightly beaten
icing sugar

Place the grape juice in a large saucepan, bring to the boil, then simmer until it has reduced down by half. Remove from the heat.

Lightly beat the egg yolks in a bowl, then pour in the grape juice, stirring continuously. Add the cream to the mixture, stir well, then pour the mix back into the saucepan through a sieve. Return the pan to the heat and cook the mixture gently until it thickens. Remove from the heat and cool. Freeze for 4 hours or until required.

Meanwhile, place the sugar in a small saucepan over a low heat and cook until it turns pale caramel in colour. Dip the little bunches of grapes in the caramel and then place them on a non-stick baking sheet on a cold surface, to set. Dust the grapes with icing sugar, arrange on top of the ice-cream and serve.

apricots

Nothing can compete with the subtle flavour of an apricot, picked straight from the tree in late summer. You'll need to grow them in a sheltered site in cold areas, ideally trained against a sunny wall. Otherwise, they must be grown in a greenhouse.

The trees themselves are hardy, but the flowers appear in late winter and are susceptible to frost damage when growing outside. To protect them, drape the branches with horticultural fleece at blossom time and leave in place until the fruits form. This will, however, keep out pollinating insects, so you will need to do this job for them with a paintbrush. Train the main shoots in a fan shape as they grow, or buy a ready-trained tree. In early summer, tie in new shoots, cutting out any that lie awkwardly. This new growth will flower and fruit next year. After harvesting, cut back shoots that have fruited.

Soil: Deep, fertile, but not too heavy.
Climate: Warm and sheltered.
Water: Water trees well during periods of drought in summer.
Harvest: Pick the fruits when fully ripe.

Apricot Ice

Preparation: 15 minutes, plus 4 hours freezing
Serves: 4–6

300 g (10 oz) ripe apricots
1 tablespoon lemon juice
mint sprigs, to garnish

Bring 500 ml (17 fl oz) water to the boil in a saucepan. Place the apricots in the water and leave for 30 seconds, then remove with a slotted spoon. Allow them to cool in a colander under cold running water, then use a knife to pull away their skin: it should slip right off. Cut the apricots down the middle and remove the stones.

Return the apricots to the water and simmer for 5 minutes. Remove and blend with the lemon juice until smooth. Pour the mixture into ice-cube trays and freeze for 4 hours.

Before serving place the ice-cube trays in a shallow dish of warm water (or a baking pan) for 10 seconds to loosen and melt slightly. Serve crammed into glasses, with a dollop of crème fraîche and a garnish of mint leaves. The cubes can also be added to cocktails and fruit juice.

Lychee and Apricot Compote

Preparation: 20 minutes, plus 1 hour chilling
Cooking: 10 minutes
Serves: 4

425 g (14 oz) canned lychees
12 apricots
2 large oranges
2 tablespoons pine nuts

Drain the lychees, reserving the liquid in a bowl. Add enough water to make the liquid up to 300 ml (10 fl oz).

Place the apricots in a large pan and pour the liquid over them. Allow them to soak for 2 minutes, then drain, reserving the liquid, and rinse the apricots under cold water. Peel off the skins and cut in half down the 'seam' of the apricot.

Return the apricots to the pan, with the reserved liquid, and bring to simmering point, stirring gently, for 10 minutes. Allow to cool.

Scoop the lychees and apricots into a large bowl and pour the liquid on top.

Pare off thin strips of orange rind with a potato peeler and cut lengthways into needle-thin strips. Peel the oranges and cut into segments, removing the membrane with a sharp knife. Add the orange segments to the bowl and gently mix together with the apricots and lychees. Set aside in the fridge for 1 hour, to chill.

Lightly toast the pine-nuts in a heavy-based frying pan. When ready to serve, transfer the fruit to serving dishes and sprinkle over the pine nuts.

figs

Figs are hardy, but to ensure a decent crop, you need to grow them in a sheltered spot – ideally trained against a warm wall – and you need to restrict the roots. Growing them in a container is usually the best method of doing this, but beware as roots dry out more quickly in a pot. Sinking your container in the ground will cut down on watering. In a warm climate, figs will produce two or three crops a year, but that is more than you can hope for where cold winters are the norm. Look for small figs on the branches in early spring. These are the ones that you will be picking in late summer. Remove larger, withered-looking fruits. Any small figs that develop in early to midsummer are best removed – they do not have time to ripen and will divert the plant's energy from the crop. Train the stems against the wall in a fan pattern as they grow. Pruning is best carried out in winter – during the growing season, sap bleeds copiously from cut stems. Cut back old branches and shorten any shoots growing away from the wall.

Soil: Fertile and well-drained. In a container, use good-quality compost and feed regularly.
Water: Water frequently during the growing season; never allow the roots to dry out.
Climate: Full sun, sheltered from strong winds. Hard winter frosts can damage embryo fruits, next year's crop.
Harvest: Late summer in temperate climates.

Yogurt and Passion Fruit Figs

Preparation: 10 minutes
Serves: 2

2 passion fruit
200 ml (7 fl oz) natural yogurt
1 tablespoon honey
4 figs, quartered
mint sprigs, to decorate

Cut each passion fruit in half, scoop out the seeds into a large bowl and mix them with the yogurt and honey, stirring well to combine.

Arrange the figs in 2 serving bowls or on plates. Spoon over the yogurt mixture and serve, decorated with mint sprigs.

recipe index

Picture credits: Alamy/Marie-Louise Avery 50 top left/Pernilla Bergdahl 114 top centre, 110 top centre/ 22 top right, 92 centre right/ 24 bottom centre/L. Frost 63 top left, 70 top centre, 85 top/Mark & Audrey Gibson back cover top right, 141 bottom left /Robert Harding World Imagery 16 bottom right/A.I.Lord 112 top centre/mediacolors 118 top centre/Kader Meguedad 79 top left/Richard Osbourne/ Blue Pearl Photographic 152 top centre/Neil Sutherland 28 centre/Matt Wicker 63 top right/Comstock Production Department 44 bottom left/Steve Hamblin 36 bottom left/Image Source 156 top centre/image100 79 bottom centre/Serge Kozak 16 bottom left/Arco/ R. Tscherwitschke 43 left, 143 centre left/David Wasserman 137 bottom left. **Octopus Publishing Group Ltd**/Michelle Garrett 5 bottom right/Jason Lowe 16 top left,70 bottom right, 107 bottom left, 150 top left/Frank Adam 8 top right, 29 bottom, 70 bottom left, 127 bottom right, 69 bottom/Jean Cazals 44 top left/Stephen Conroy 36 top right, 150 top right/Jeremy Hopley 44 top right, 50 top right, 62 bottom centre/David Jordan 43 right, 141 bottom right, 147/Graham Kirk 26 main/Sandra Lane 8 top left, 22 left/William Lingwood back cover top left, 85 bottom left/David Loftus front cover left, 8 bottom right, 79 top right, 83 main, 95/Neil Mersh 5 bottom left, 74 main, 117 main, 139 main/James Murray 16 top right/William Reavell back cover top centre, 22 bottom right, 36 top left, 44 bottom right, 127 bottom left/Ian Wallace 3 centre, 85 bottom right, 89 main, 90 main, 92 left, 107 right, 137 bottom right/Philip Webb 50 bottom. **Getty Images**/David Prince 3 left, 6 Main Picture.